ge new building (artist unknown)

Harrogate College

1893–1973

DOROTHY HEWLETT

Mr G M Savery

Miss Jones

Miss Jacob

Miss Todd

Harrogate College

1893–1973

DOROTHY HEWLETT

Published by Harrogate College

Published by Harrogate College
Clarence Drive, Harrogate
North Yorkshire

© 1981 Dorothy Hewlett

ISBN 0 9507427 0 8

Printed in Great Britain by
Watmoughs Limited,
Idle, Bradford, West Yorkshire BD10 8NL

Contents

List of illustrations

Message from the Headmistress and President of the Harrogate College Union

It has been for me a privilege and great pleasure to read before publication this account of the history and life of the College from its foundation until the end of 1973. I am happy to commend it to pupils and staff, past and present, and to all friends of the College, for it gives a unique picture of our school at every stage in its development, reflecting also the social and cultural changes in the world beyond it. We are deeply indebted to Miss Hewlett for her thorough and painstaking work; no other person was so admirably qualified to do us this service. I am sure that reading and re-reading this book will prove as absorbing, amusing and rewarding to everyone as it has been to me. Its success and welcome are assured.

J. C. LAWRANCE

Harrogate College

Foreword

As I read through this history of Harrogate College I was reminded of some words from the monograph of 1959 written in commemoration of Miss Jones' ninetieth birthday: "The tradition of piety, learning and service which the School has built up since the beginning of the century". What a splendid tradition and how well it has been maintained by our headmistresses Miss Jones, Miss Jacob, Miss Todd and now Mrs Lawrance.

Many of us will remember Miss Jones' fervent wish that we should have a chapel, as she felt it was "so vital to the work", and how determined were the efforts made by everyone to make her wish a reality. Our academic achievements have always been good and the broadest view of learning has been maintained by provision for the talents of all girls and by readiness to adapt to worthwhile changes in education. Service for others has been part of our tradition from the far off days of the Kotady collection to the many and varied schemes of today.

School had its lighter side too, as we are reminded in many of its recollections. There is great joy in remembering the time when we were at school, the friends we made, the successes and perhaps some failures, the expeditions, the lectures, the lessons, the Chapel services, the serious times and the hilarious.

But so much might have been forgotten had it not been for this splendid work that has kept it for us and for our successors. That we have this history with its meticulous research and detail is due to Miss Hewlett who has been part of the School for so many years. How fortunate we are to have her as chronicler, for she has noted and remembered people, places and events, and linked them all together. We are reminded first of the early unpretentious start in Ripon Road, the move to Percy Lodge, and, as numbers increased, the final arrival in Clarence Drive. Then there was the austerity period of the 1914-18 war, to be followed by further developments during the time leading up to the evacuation from Harrogate in 1939. After that came the years at Swinton and the subsequent return, resettlement and adjustment to altered circumstances. They were dramatic changes at times, but the spirit and aims of the School have remained steadfast.

How vividly it is told and how immensely grateful we are to Miss Hewlett. We give her our heartfelt thanks for all the time she has spent and the care she has taken in producing this excellent, detailed, comprehensive and enjoyable history of the School.

SYBIL MURRAY

Introduction

The record of the life of a school as young as Harrogate College cannot be expected to contribute to the history of education in the same way as can some of the boys' schools, many of them of ancient foundation. Nevertheless the eighty years covered by this story span a period that was of great importance in the education of girls, a time when much pioneer work was being done, and when we were progressing steadily from the days of the dame's school through to the era when *Women's lib* became a common slogan, and *Equality of opportunity* a burning issue.

Much of the material for the account covering the early part of Miss Jones' headship, and before, has been gathered from the magazines of the College when it began as a boys' school, and from the early *Chronicles*, often written so vividly, and in language which in itself conveys so perfectly the atmosphere of the time that it would be a mistake not to give some of the extracts in their original form. I had hoped to have Miss Jacob's help in writing about her seventeen years, including the unique event of the evacuation to Swinton, but sadly this was not to be. Miss Todd has supplied much general information, including comments on the trends in education in the country as a whole when changes were assailing us on all sides. She also has considerable knowledge of the time when the College was changing from a private school to one with a Board of Governors, since in her early days as headmistress she frequently visited Miss Jones at Eastbourne and there was told the whole unusual story of how it came about. She and I have spent many interesting hours researching into past records and indeed sections of the book are as much her writing as mine. This I gratefully acknowledge.

All the main information on events, buildings and personnel have, I hope, been included, but I have also tried to recount happenings, not always of great importance afterwards, but at the time amusing and sometimes illuminating, which may interest those who have been in some ways closely linked with the School. Many, whether girls, teachers or onlookers, would perhaps, like me, be sorry if the passage of time meant that this history should be lost to posterity.

My personal qualification for writing the book is that all my years of teaching have been spent in Harrogate College, spanning the reign of three headmistresses. Apologies must be given for omitting some incidents which former girls may recollect as very important, and for only being able to mention individual people as they have stood out in my memory. For those who would like to delve deeper, there are many interesting bound volumes of *Chronicles* in the College, and these give, far more than this book is able to do, a fascinating record of how traditions were formed and how the School progressed towards the position of renown that it now holds in the country.

D. HEWLETT

Miss Jones' Headship

1898–1914

EARLY BEGINNINGS

The original Harrogate College was a boys' school in Ripon Road and the first records we have of it are from the School magazines of about 1890. Mr George Mearns Savery had been the headmaster for about ten years and the School was flourishing under his direction and appears to have been an independent school for about eighty boys, some of whom were boarders. The premises were a substantial stone building with a tower and battlements on Ripon Road near to the present Cairn Hotel, and there are references to dinner parties in the Majestic Hotel opposite. Behind the school there was a playing field of considerable size stretching to what is now Clarence Drive. There seems to have been a few houses in Duchy Road and Ripon Road but wide areas of open country formed most of the environment.

Mr Savery was evidently very well esteemed in Harrogate and a very successful headmaster who at that time would be about forty years of age. There is an interesting copy, still extant, of *Rules for the Boys' College* in 1893 and it now makes amusing reading. Some extracts are quoted:

Boots must be put on before breakfast and taken off before evening school. All are expected to wear slippers during evening school and to keep their feet still.

Free conversation is allowed in the dining room but not loud talking or laughter. Reading while eating is forbidden. On leaving the room pupils are expected to bow to the master on duty.

On Sundays no playing or reading unsuitable books is allowed. No talking is allowed going to and from church (Trinity Wesley). All must keep step and walk behind the leaders.

There are thirty fines listed, including the following:

For neglecting to throw the bedclothes away from the bed on rising	½d
For meddling with the gas lights	1d
For letting soap, flannel etc choke the bath waste pipe	3d
For throwing paper on the floor	½d
For kicking a cap on the playground	1d
For losing the copy of the rules	2d

G M Savery
headmaster

1893 the Boys' School, Schoolroom

A few of the Old Boys of Harrogate College were able to be present at a re-union in 1948 and there are probably sons and daughters in Harrogate who remember accounts of their fathers' life at the school.

In 1893 Mr Savery decided to open a small school for sisters and other girls and he rented a building now known as Dirlton Lodge on Ripon Road for the purpose. The first headmistress was Miss Field-Hall and the only photograph that we have of her is one taken with some of her girls which is now displayed in one of the College corridors. After two years the School was moved to a better building called Percy Lodge close to Trinity Wesley Church and between the Leeds and Otley Roads. This building was commodious and had a hall and enough rooms for the teaching and housing of both boarding and day girls in an expanding school. Miss Field-Hall was evidently greatly liked by her girls and much regret was expressed when she gave up the headship and sought another post in 1898. By this time Mr Savery realised that the

Harrogate Ladies' College was a successful venture (we note that the fees per term for tuition were £6) and he required to appoint a headmistress who would assist him in this pioneer work for girls. Thus began the thirty-seven years of Miss Jones' headship working for her first few years under the direction and inspiration of Mr Savery of the Boys' School.

An account of how Miss Jones came to be appointed at an early age is given by Miss Davies in her monograph written in 1959 on the occasion of Miss Jones' ninetieth birthday and it is appropriate to quote from it. "The story may fitly begin in the year 1891 when Elizabeth Wilhelmina Jones at the age

1899 The first Headmistress, Miss Field-Hall, with a group of her old girls

of twenty-two took her degree, graduating at the Royal University of Ireland (Queen's College, Belfast). Almost immediately she set forth across the sea to England to begin her life work at her chosen profession of teaching. It so happened that on one of her visits to the Educational Agency in 1893 Miss M E Roberts, the headmistress of the noted Bradford Girls' Grammar School, was interviewing candidates for positions on her staff, and she consented to see the young Miss Jones. So began the five years of happy and fruitful work under the leadership of Miss Roberts, wise, scholarly and extremely able, which culminated in 1898 when the scene changed to Harrogate." While in Bradford Miss Jones evidently began to apply for headships, and one of her applications was brought to the notice of Mr Savery who eventually offered her the headship of Harrogate Ladies' College. Miss Davies continues: "For some time Miss Jones hesitated. A small private school, as it was then, was not regarded as giving great scope for development, and a period of painful indecision followed. A quiet weekend spent by her and a great friend and colleague at their holiday cottage at Grassington in Wharfedale brought the final decision. Miss Jones often told how they walked together, and her friend said firmly "When we reach that gate you must answer yes or no". Just as they reached the gate, lo and behold, a small shining object lay on the ground—a little horseshoe shamrock brooch. "Yes" said Miss Jones, and the letter was written to Mr Savery that night. Thus in September 1898 Miss Jones became headmistress of the College, then in its infancy at Percy Lodge." Mention of Grassington is a reminder that nearly fifty years later a house was bought in Clarence Drive for the headmistress, and Miss Jones, when asked to name it, chose *Grassington*, and so it has remained.

Several girls who were to become well known in the College annals were at Percy Lodge, among them Marian Talbot (Auty) who sent her daughter Mary (Kingswell) to school, the first of the second generation of pupils, and Mary in her turn sent Josephine (Bankes) to be the first of the third generation. Birdie Brailsford (Booth) went to Dartford for physical training and sent her girls Margaret and Dorothy to the College and four grand-daughters followed. Dorothy Watson (Woodhead) coming slightly later had her daughter Margaret (Chary) at school, followed by Carolyn (Sutherland), and her daughter Deborah, entering in 1977, has become the first of the fourth generation. Norah Manson went to Newnham and later returned to teach languages, and Edith Barraclough was the first Union secretary in those early days. Pre-eminent among the Percy Lodge girls in her contribution to the development of the College was Louie Davies who became the private secretary and confidante of Miss Jones, and was her devoted friend and admirer throughout her life. Her outstanding musicianship and love of literature permeated the School, and her influence was second only to that of the headmistress. It was she who established the School's musical tradition, and her literary talents found scope in the School *Chronicle* which she edited with conspicuous flair until her retirement in 1940.

One or two extracts from records of these early days give an indication of how the young school was establishing itself as a community.

One pupil, F M Dale, wrote later of her early memories at Percy Lodge in 1895: "On 25 January a heavy snow storm came on and the time afterwards was one of the keenest frosts known. Everything was frozen. The gas lights went off and we had to do our work by the light of candles and go to bed by the blaze of our bedroom fires (no hot pipes in those days). Water we had none for several weeks except what was handed over the wall in buckets from the convent next door. We went skating every day. There were no games played then by girls, even in good weather, just a little weak tennis in the summer. The Old Girls' Union had just been started but its attendance was very small and I only remember the presence of three Old Girls. There was an epidemic of 'flu throughout the country. Every morning we were given a pill as a preventive and we called them 'Faith Pills' but nearly every girl got the 'flu all the same. All regular work came to an end and Percy Lodge assumed the habits of a hospital. It must have been rather tiresome to keep it going. I was sent to learn Shelley's *Cloud* by heart during this period, and I can remember most of it yet. During the summer term of 1895 we had some lectures from Mr Savery on Lord Macaulay, illustrated by recitations from the *Lays*. The prize-giving was the great event of the summer term. It was held in the Harlow Manor Hydro in Cold Bath Road to which we went many times in advance to practise for the concert—a fine affair of new white frocks and bouquets.''

The Whit holiday 1901: "The day before Whit Monday Miss Jones announced that we should have a holiday, which news was received with hearty and continuous applause. Some girls spent the day with friends but the rest went in brakes to Brimham Rocks, a distance of about ten miles, the road being hilly all the way. We started about 9 30 in three carriages. The horse in the last chariot showed a marked affection for the inhabitants of the one in front and alarmed them considerably by more than once putting its head in their midst. The road looked very pretty as we passed along, wild flowers being abundant, violets and bluebells colouring the banks on either side.''

"The last two miles or so of the road is extremely stiff and along the path which leads up to the rocks the soil is soft and sandy. We arrived about 11 30 and had lunch out in the open and then set off to explore those wonderful rocks which are said to be the finest and most remarkable to be found in England. They are all shapes and sizes, some just resting on the slightest ledges. During the afternoon a heavy shower came on so we had to take shelter in the one small cottage up on the rocks and had tea in a little barn. We bought some lilac at a house in Ripley and went away rejoicing with our spoil, at the same time feeling we had helped a good cause as the lady said she would put the money in the missionary box. We got back to Percy Lodge about 7 30, after the two hours' very pleasant ride home.''

A holiday in 1903: "The fact that we were to have a holiday came as a pleasant surprise, for the announcement was not made until after the second lesson. After a considerable delay we set off, to the number of about sixty, in two wagonettes, a large brake and a landau, the cavalcade being led by a four-in-hand with the horn very much in evidence. First we drove off from the Oval (Percy Lodge) to the College (the boys' school) where we were joined by Mr and Mrs Savery, and after setting off again we went round by the new Ladies' College which is growing apace, and away to Plumpton Rocks for our picnic.''

Old Girls 1902: "On Saturday 5 July the Old Girls' Union had its annual excursion, but although there were only nineteen members present we had a very enjoyable day and went on horse coaches to Fountains Abbey. At the business meeting which took place at tea at Hill House Farm Miss Jones read the financial statement, and after all expenses had been paid there was a balance of £2 7s 5d and this was voted to be donated to the Harrogate Ladies' College Dramatic Society. A vote of thanks was given to Miss Hammond for the excellent help she had been since the foundation of the Union, and Edith Barraclough was elected as the new secretary.''

Old Girls 1903: Miss Jones writes "I am glad that this year the Union reached the number of fifty-six members. The terms of the subscription are placed as low as the expenses will allow, 1/- per annum without the magazine and 2/6 per annum with the magazine which is issued three times a year. The magazine contains news of old girls as well as an account of current school events. As it is chiefly through the magazine that we are able to maintain the interest of the old girls in the school we hope that most of the members will be 2/6 subscribers."

It seems appropriate to quote at this point an extract from a speech given by Miss Jones at the HCU meeting of 1956 while recalling former days:

"I feel very grateful that so much trouble has been taken to arrange that our meeting should take place here [in the North Dining Room which was the former assembly hall of the school]. The link which has been formed to unite members of the Union in whatever part of the world they may meet is not felt more strongly anywhere than in this spot. What is this link? How was it formed and how maintained? Venturing on definition, I would say it is a shared feeling of love, loyalty and gratitude to the school, and to the friendships that are formed in the dear companionship of school days and remain life long. This link began to be formed in the now distant past sixty years ago when a few school friends met together, and it was strengthened year by year as these gatherings gradually grew larger. About 1900 the gathering took on a more formal character and it was proposed that we should draw up a constitution, formulate our rules, express our ideals and give a precise aim and purpose to our Old Girls' organisation—in fact give ourselves a charter."

"I came across my own notes of this meeting this spring. I had noted an awareness among our members that a new era of greatly enlarged opportunity for women had just dawned. Our founder had spoken of it and had indeed founded our school in anticipation of its needs. We have seen the full tide of that era, sweeping women into almost every career and profession in the last fifty years. The discussion that followed turned on the qualities that a woman would need to enable her to meet the challenge of such an age. It was agreed that there should be no discrimination, either on social or sectarian lines, but that the enlightened and tolerant spirit our school had tried to teach should be carried into later intercourse with our fellow human beings in those wider fields that were opening on all sides. It was further agreed that members should aim at being helpful to others in life, especially to school companions who found themselves in need or difficulty, and that at all times a strong effort should be made to reach in our own personal lives a high standard of truth, duty, loyalty and good manners. With such high ideals our Old Girls' Association grew up: no harm is done by reminding ourselves of them every now and then."

Miss Jones went on to recall another meeting some years later, when some of the members declared themselves affronted by being referred to as *Old Girls* and they felt the Union should at once assume a more worthy title. At that meeting the offending words *Old Girls* were dropped and *Harrogate College Union* became from that day the official name. Miss Jones concluded "By recalling these two meetings one gets an idea of the evolution of the Union from infancy to maturity, for one can see how the link was formed and grew."

THE NEW SCHOOL

About 1900 Mr Savery began to plan a new building for the Ladies' College using as the site the part of the boys' playing fields which bordered on Clarence Drive. He had expert advice, and Miss Jones also is known to have visited Cheltenham to consult Miss Beale. An ecstatic comment written in 1902 by one of the Percy Lodge girls reflects the excitement with which the coming move was anticipated by pupils.

"The new school is begun! And pinning our faith in the old saying 'well begun is half done' we feel that the consummation of our hopes is really coming within reach. We look forward to a land of promise, an Arcadia, an Eldorado. This difficulty will be done away with, that trouble will be avoided, the other enjoyment will be enhanced—all will go smoothly, happily and successfully in work and play—when we get into the new school. And certainly if convenience of arrangements, care, wisdom, and kind consideration on the part of those in whose hands the enterprise lies, can bring about the fulfilment of these hopes, fulfilled they will be. It only remains for us, as our share of the enterprise, to see that what we contribute to the new school shall be worthy of it."

The (boys') school magazines of that date report how Mr and Mrs Savery were to be seen daily supervising every stage of the building. The new school was completed in 1904 and on 17 May of that year the flag was hoisted and the Percy Lodge girls moved in. Mr Savery and his wife remained closely associated with the girls' school, and Miss Jones, then about thirty, was headmistress under Mr Savery's direction.

By this time more help was needed, and names famous in the school's life begin to be noticed on the staff. Miss Jones' sister Lena was already playing a lively part in the drama and games. In 1904 Miss Violet Gask joined the staff with high qualifications to teach English and Latin and to be second in command, which post she held until her retirement in 1936. Miss Gent who also came at this time spent thirty years in the school, and Miss Bronte as matron was in charge for many years. Lena's friend from Ireland, Dora Forde, came initially "to help" in a variety of ways. Later she was to become housemistress of Lincoln and along with her close associate Louie Davies she was one of the more outstanding pioneers.

The main school block exists today very much as it was then in 1904, but it will be of interest to give some account of the use of the rooms as was first planned. One has to realise that the whole school of some eighty boarders and forty day girls all lived and worked in the new school.

On the ground floor facing the front was the school dining room, and behind it the kitchens (unaltered until 1946). Miss Jones had her drawing room and dining room on one side of the entrance and on the other was a very small staff room, two class rooms and a beautiful well-lit and comfortably furnished drawing room for the girls. This room later became the school library, but until it was altered in 1922 there were no common rooms as now called, and Miss Jones used this room to meet the girls, and to read to them while they did their needlework. At the back of the school was the fine lecture hall

B

entered by some glass doors from the entrance hall. Later these doors were removed to make room for the mahogany doors given by Lord Davidson, but the original conception of leaded glass doors and windows opening onto the lecture room from the entrance passages was very distinctive and attractive. There was a good spring floor in the big room, reached by some circular steps, and also at one end a small platform for use for Prayers and concerts. Along the inner wall were four "boxes" similar to those still in use at Harrogate Royal Hall. These were used by Miss Jones and her family and by the senior members of staff for assemblies and lectures, and gave a splendid vantage point on such occasions. In 1906 after Mr Savery's death a small organ was placed on the platform in his memory and Miss Davies spent her early years in that room and on that organ in building up the choir's musical reputation. It was only after the chapel was completed that this very beautiful little organ was removed and sold. The distinctive "boxes" remained until the hall was converted into a permanent dining room but the relics of them can still be seen, and the wooden railings which replaced them inside the North Dining Room must sometimes mystify present day occupants. On the east side of the main building was a hard playground and considerable grass and trees, and there was a small one-storey gymnasium with a good stage for dramatic work.

Original Assembly Hall (N dining room) showing organ and staff boxes

On the first floor of the school over the entrance hall was the original library. In 1910 the girls, assisted by the proceeds of a pageant, gave a set of oak bookcases to the room, and the old girls gave an overmantel for the fireplace depicting Sir Percivale's vision of the Holy Grail. When eventually this room became York common room the House inherited a very finely furnished room with ample accommodation for their belongings. Also on the first floor but facing the back playing fields was the original science room with benches and water and gas. In this room for many years after I joined the staff in 1920 was taught all the physics, chemistry and botany. Next door was the art room, and when Miss Jones went to Italy for her holidays she would bring back replicas of famous statuaries, busts and pictures, thus making it a place full of inspiration and ideas. All the school and class rooms had pictures everywhere. In the main lower corridor was a full size Venus de Milo, and in the entrance hall a Winged Victory. For many years after the removal of the statues the position of the prefect on duty in the corridor was still referred to as "on Venus" which must have frequently puzzled the school. Many of the older Old Girls may wonder what happened to all the pictures and objects of art which adorned the corridors: these were, alas, some of the losses of the second world war. When the College was hurriedly evacuated all such property had to be left behind. No one knows what happened to them. The Venus was to be seen (painted yellow) in one of the gardens in a small street in Harrogate for a year or two, and the art room busts are said to have formed rubble under the new exit drive from the school. It is very sad to think that so many beautiful things, collected with such care, came to this end in circumstances outside our control.

The rest of the school's original building was used as class rooms and bedrooms for the girls. Miss Jones had her bedroom at the end of the first floor corridor and Mrs Savery, after her husband's death, had her room beside her: this room later, on the return from the war, became the York housemistress's room. Part of the second floor, later called Lancaster, was the sick wing and was still so called for many years later.

With this accommodation and with two small rooms in the "stables" for cookery, and some practical work, and with the fine large boys' playing field at the back to share at stated times for hockey, tennis, and later cricket, the original Ladies' College had everything it could need for a first class and much sought after boarding school.

Extracts from the *Girls' Realm* 1904 by L Ruggles Roberts and the *Harrogate Advertiser* by "Free Lance" in 1904 are quoted:

"Harrogate, long famed for its waters, bids fair to become equally celebrated for its colleges, but of all the institutions for the training of the young none possesses a more promising future than the Ladies' College. In May of this year possession was taken of the present imposing buildings in Clarence Drive. The greatest number of boarders that the building can accommodate is ninety, and the maximum is attained.

"It is a very handsome exterior that the College presents to the onlooker, surrounded by eight acres of ground, beautifully laid out. The interior arrangements justify the promise of the building. Here all is charming. From

Venus de Milo in School corridor

the moment of one's entrance into the picturesque solid oak square hall with its carpet soft to the feet, one is impressed by the prevailing note of colour and daintiness. The delicate soft shades of green, yellow and white that reveal themselves everywhere embody the old traditions of the House Beautiful and put to shame the superabundant decorations and furnishing which seem to be so common among both the middle and the upper classes. Everywhere down to the class rooms the student's eye finds repose in the green panels, and most of the desks are made of pine, tinted dark green. They are known as Dr Roth's hygienic desks and contain a pad for the support of the pupil's back which may be adjusted to any height. The desk too may be lifted up or down and brought nearer to the pupil, which all prevents the student from stooping or becoming round-shouldered.

"In the tour of the school with the headmistress we came to a series of little rooms with glass panels in the doors and peering through I saw a piano in each. In response to a bell, thirteen sweet maidens trooped up with music portfolios under their arms. They glided into the little rooms and, in less time than it takes to write it, thirteen pianos were engaged in thirteen different tunes: the sound would have been deafening, but these rooms were sound proof and the next door neighbour could not be heard.

"Free Lance" writes "We followed my guide into a fine room looking out onto the playground which was the girls' drawing room, well lighted and delicately furnished. We went up the wide carpeted stairs, stopping before delicious little alcoves, the windows of which overlooked the large cricket ground at the rear and from which miles and miles of wood and pasture-land could be seen in the hazy distance. On the walls of the passages were framed historical facsimiles of notable letters from the reign of Henry VIII down to Queen Victoria. 'You would be surprised' said Miss Jones 'how interesting the girls find these pictures, not only in the incidents to which they relate but they see for themselves the writing of the celebrities, the style of spelling, and the progress which literature generally has made from reign to reign'. A fine array of pictures and autotypes of ancient and modern art find a place in corridors and rooms. The large dining room contains not stern reprehensible pieces of mahogany but a number of little tables on which were vases of flowers supplied by the pupils themselves: it reminded one more of the table d'hôte of a hotel than a school. The College has been able to adopt all the latest appliances of hygienic theory that are in vogue. The rooms are ventilated by air shafts communicating with Boyle's patent Air Pump Ventilators on the roof. The building is lighted by electricity and heated by hot water radiators, though these are supplemented by open fires in the larger living rooms, bedrooms and class rooms.

"For indoor exercise the girls, one and all, partake of drill, and one mistress, specially trained by Madame Bergman Osterberg, is in charge of the gymnasium. Excess is guarded against and interest sustained by the record of weights and heights which is kept. As two to four hours daily are spent in the open air, outdoor games are a prominent feature of school life. There are tennis and croquet lawns and the rest of the ground is divided between the devotees of hockey, vigoro, basket ball and cricket. The school costume consists of a green coat and skirt, white blouse and white sailor hat with the hat band of school colours and badge.

"The influence of the headmistress is backed by an ingenious arrangement which so acts that the best-charactered girls in the school take the lead. This is provided for by the selection of Prefects by the staff for good conduct, and the influence they exert on the moral tone of the school is very great.

"With a headmistress who takes so personal an interest in the pupils under her charge, with a staff so admirably qualified for its work, with buildings so modern and a situation so bracing and healthgiving as Harrogate, the College is coming to be recognised as an establishment in the first rank for the grafting and fruition of that triad of distinctions the modern woman aims at—grace, culture and honour."

21

b

With the school so happily established in its new premises and looking forward to a future full of promise, it must have been a tragedy of great magnitude when in 1905 Mr Savery became so seriously ill that he felt it necessary to hand over the running of the boys' school to his Senior Master. Presumably in doing this he hoped he might still be able to supervise both schools for some years, but after a time of convalescence at Grange-over-Sands he died at the early age of fifty five. Sadly the original boys' school did not long survive after his death and with its closure the girls' school legally assumed the name of Harrogate College. Miss Jones lost a great friend and adviser and the scene darkened. In building the school Mr Savery had risked all of his resources, and there were periods of financial anxiety and stringency. His brother, Mr Servington Savery, later MP for Scarborough, was for many years on the committee, and Mrs Savery spent much of her time at the College giving invaluable advice and help, during her nineteen years of widowhood, until she died in 1924. By the terms of Mr Savery's will, Miss Jones was given the right to purchase, in his wife's lifetime, up to half of the school at cost price: on his wife's death she was to inherit one quarter outright with the option of purchasing the remaining quarter.

Tributes to Mr Savery: In the *Harrogate Herald,* 1905 Mr W H Breare wrote: "Harrogate has suffered an inestimable loss by the death of George Mearns Savery after a long illness. The lamented gentleman was one of those rare personalities to whom communities involuntarily turn for guidance, encouragement and support. Like many men of intellectual strength and practical minds the keynote of his nature was simplicity. Ever dignified and courteous in his bearing he possessed that innate kindliness and sympathy of heart which lent weight and conviction to his counsels. Gifted with oratorial powers and cultured reasoning, he was often able, on public platforms, to render signal service to many deserving causes. During the early history of the Yorkshire Home for Incurables, when it needed the sympathy and financial aid of the public to enable it to embark on a wider sphere of work, he was steadfast in support of its developments: to the Harrogate Literary Society he proved himself, indeed, their guide, philosopher and friend.

"My Savery came to Harrogate in 1885 to undertake the direction of the College, Ripon Road. Under his administration the pupils increased and the work soon rose to a high scholastic level and he was one of the first to become impressed with the disproportionate opportunities for intellectual culture available to girlhood, resulting in the establishment of the Ladies' College in Clarence Drive. Nor were Mr Savery's labours confined to his own schools. He was chairman of the Harrogate School Board and occupied a seat on the town council where he was highly regarded as a colleague. In the year before he died he was invited to become parliamentary Liberal candidate for Ealing, London."

One of Mr Savery's old boys, Sir Bertrand Watson, MP for Stockton and a chief metropolitan magistrate and a governor of the College paid this tribute: "It seems to me that my whole life was influenced by three men, one of them G M Savery, my headmaster from the age of eleven to seventeen at Harrogate College. He was a powerful personality and one to whom the term disciplinarian could be applied, but in him we saw the ideal of perfect justice being lived up to most successfully. Strict though he was I never heard a boy complain of his judgment, and all who passed through the College must have gone out into the world with the conviction that if they were fair and just it would indeed be difficult for the world to speak ill of them. Savery had been president of the Oxford Union when Asquith was at the University and when I mentioned his name, somewhere about 1920, an immediate and genuine interest was shown by the great statesman even in spite of the passage of years.''

An extract from an old copy of *The Methodist Recorder* gives further insight into Mr Savery's character. It was called "Recalling Vivid Christmas Memories of the Eighties", and was by T Driffield Hawkin, an "old boy" of the original Harrogate College.

"I saw little of my native town, for I was at my last school in Harrogate during our stay there. The master there was Mearns Savery, who later founded the great Harrogate Ladies' College. He had a great and gracious influence on my life, and to him I owe all my interest in public affairs, without which I should have been a wage-earner and not a human being, for I had no particular aptitude in life. Among other things, he took me to my first political meeting before the Christmas holidays. The election contest raged about Gladstone's Home Rule Bill, which broke up the Liberal Party and the non-conformist conscience. The meeting was at the little Harrogate Town Hall to welcome the Unionist candidate, who sat in the midst of his supporters, including my master, at a table on the projecting stage. Behind them was the large theatre curtain, which could be drawn apart for plays.

"I was seated close to the door, and did not find things exciting there. So I wandered up to the stage to inspect some of the properties assembled for the Christmas pantomime due in a fortnight. I could hear the speaking and the applause, and suddenly noticed a large Union Jack attached to a long pole leaning against the wall, and I had an inspiration the flag should appear and wave as the candidate finished his speech. How excited I was, as I stood there waiting for the applause; for so far as my politics went I was on his side. The moment came, and I pushed the flag through the curtain and was rewarded by hearing the applause become a roar. When I was seized by an angry curator—was he a Radical?—a brief struggle ensued, and the standard dropped suddenly on the candidate and his supporters, enveloping them all amid picturesque confusion. But the candidate improved the occasion when he crawled out, by wrapping himself in it. I was hauled out, crestfallen, by the savage official, and reported to Mr Savery, whose eyes, however, twinkled as he heard the horrid story. He said to me afterwards that my entry into politics had been suitable to my age, and he could not find it a cause for punishment.

"So I came home for my Christmas holidays, proud of my political strategy. This little story could illustrate many aspects of life, one being the value of wisdom and tolerance toward the young.''

Extract from Old Girls' meeting in 1906: "After the ordinary business, Mrs Booth, better known as B Brailsford, placed before the meeting a very interesting proposal, namely, that an oil painting of the founder of the Ladies'

College should be presented to the school. This motion was unanimously carried, and Louie Davies, the local secretary, undertook to receive subscriptions. The painting would cost £50.

"On 14 November, 1906 a beautiful two manual organ which had been erected in the school lecture hall to the memory of the founder, was opened by Sir Frederick Bridge, organist of Westminster Abbey, conductor of the London Choral Society. This organ was used until 1923, when the new organ in memory of Mrs Savery was placed in the chapel."

Dorothy Fargus, a pupil in 1906 wrote in the *Chronicle*: "One of the greatest events in the early years of the College was the building and opening of the beautiful organ in memory of the founder. In the autumn term we had the great pleasure of welcoming Sir Frederick Bridge. For weeks beforehand we were all practising the special hymn and other choral items for the concert. After prayers had been offered by the vicar of St Wilfrids, the Rev W F Swann, we had the great pleasure of an organ recital by 'Westminster Bridge' as he was sometimes called."

On Mr Savery's death the main responsibility for the school fell on Miss Jones. Fortunately she was to have the support and advice of Mrs Savery and Mr Servington Savery, and she herself was generous in her acknowledgement of their help. It is evident from the records that the Ladies' College was soon doing very well indeed: its reputation was high, there was considerable pressure for entry, and although the main building of 1904 was thought to provide all that was necessary, only a few years elapsed before more space was needed for its growing numbers, and it is noted in the *Chronicle* of 1907 "we are greatly looking forward to the time when the new wing will be ready for use".

The new wing was a three-storey block built behind the one-storey gymnasium. The ground floor provided three cloakrooms and above these were six classrooms which looked out onto the field at the back. An additional little room was, in those days, given over to the craft of bookbinding, in charge of an enthusiastic teacher (one or two relics of her craft still survive). The name, the "Bindery" persisted long after the change of function, and must have often puzzled newcomers to the school. It was obvious that this block was only the beginning of the extension designed to be completed at some later date, and this did indeed occur in 1925. An extract from the record of 1907 reports "The day pupils are to be provided with a cloakroom to themselves and they will benefit even more than the boarders by their new quarters after the very uncomfortable life they have led in the narrow passage which was their only cloakroom. One great advantage of the new premises will be that the library, the art and the science rooms on the first floor corridor will no longer also be required as form rooms. The new wing is to be erected at the cost of £2 000." It is of interest to note that two years later in 1909 it was decided to discontinue the day section of over sixty girls, the College thus becoming a school for boarders only.

A notice concerning the opening of a branch school near Paris appears about this time. "In September 1907 a school will be opened under Miss Gimblett to be worked as a branch of the Ladies' College where elder girls may go for a time to acquire a conversational knowledge of French and take lessons in Paris in art, music etc. at the Sorbonne. The girls will be accompanied on walks and excursions by French mistresses and young French girls. The Maison Blanche is a comfortable house close to the Forest of St Germain, about half an hour from Paris. The domestic arrangements will be as nearly as possible like those of the Ladies' College. One day a week will be a whole holiday to afford an opportunity for sight seeing in Paris. French will be spoken at all times except for a short interval on Sundays. Miss Gimblett has been associated with the Ladies' College for over eight years and she has our very good wishes for success in her new sphere of work." From time to time accounts are written in the *Chronicle* about the Maison Blanche, and it evidently formed a very successful and happy ending to many girls' school life. It seems that the school was closed in 1914 at the outbreak of the war and internal arrangements were then made at the College for a French finishing department which continued for several years.

LIFE AT COLLEGE
IN THE EARLY YEARS

The *Chronicles* are full of references to the half-holidays which were a feature of each term. As was her wont to the end, Miss Jones loved to announce an unexpected day's outing and enjoyed these herself to the full: she was a keen walker and the girls were often taken for very long expeditions. Brimham Rocks is frequently described and this entailed a walk to the railway station, train to Dacre in the Nidd Valley, and then a long three-mile walk uphill to the rocks for the picnic, with the return the same way. Fountains Abbey had to be reached by train to Ripon, followed by the walk through Studley Park to the ruins. Bolton was visited by train and then brakes to the abbey, with a walk by the Wharfe to Strid Cottage and back: anyone who has done this round will know it needed much stamina. Great Almscliffe was often a venue and the village of Birstwith with its bluebell woods was another favourite. When I myself arrived at school these holidays were often a lovely surprise and I remember one to Leyburn in Wensleydale, this time in open chara-bancs, when all the school were put down to walk on Leyburn Shawl, follow-ing Miss Jones who led the way. But the school found the Shawl and its views less interesting than the village with its shops, and Miss Jones' wrath was quite unbounded when she discovered as she reached her goal that her com-panions were only a few members of staff, who were roundly scolded for not supervising the girls to more effect.

Another time it was Rievaulx, on a hot day, in open buses, over the dusty lanes of Yorkshire, when almost every girl arrived with streaming eyes and took little heed of Rievaulx Terrace, particularly so when it was found that the lorry with the picnic hampers had lost its way and was much delayed on arrival. A story was also told of a much earlier visit to Rievaulx when a thunderstorm soaked everyone to the skin and Miss Jones and Miss Gask bought up every vest in the village shops so that the girls could don a garment while their blouses were dried by the owner of the Inn which was providing

1913 en route for Rievaulx

tea. There is also a reference to the Whit Monday outing in 1903 when the girls went to Hackfalls on the river Ure near Masham. Describing this there is the first reference to Swinton Hall, later to become so much part of the story of the school. It had been purchased some years previously by Mr Samuel Cunliffe-Lister, the well-known silk manufacturer of Bradford, who had become Baron Masham in 1891. This house, which became his country seat, lies to the south of the town on the way to Hackfalls, so the girls were able to get a good view of it without leaving the carriages. Miss Jones may have remembered this outing when she came back in 1939 to help to establish the school in what was to be its wartime home.

The school concerts, often held every month, were evidently the highlights of each term, and the programmes are given in full in the *Chronicles*. Some of the performers mentioned there are still remembered. Margareta Webster (Eastwood), Josephine Talbot, the great aunt of Josephine Kingswell (now HCU governor) and Cathie Cauldwell who later taught at Oakdale and College.

Sometimes these concerts were given in aid of the school charities, particularly for Kotady, a mission school in Ceylon. This name is still perpetuated as referring to the charities as a whole, although the actual mission has long since ended. It is interesting to note, too, that St Wilfrid's Church is mentioned in 1907, when the Rev W F Swann, the first vicar of the temporary hall then used as the church, thanked the girls for the gift of an altar frontal.

The following extract about the music and the choir was written by Miss Davies in 1909: "As time goes on it is interesting to pause now and again to review the events of former days as the choir has slowly but steadily enlarged its boundaries in different directions. Four years ago there was no choir. Then the first small beginnings appeared when six girls, stationed in different parts of the hall 'led' the singing, often alone but always undismayed, rescuing the hymn or psalm from untimely and ignominious collapse. Even the advent of the organ failed at first to give the stimulus that was expected, but gradually more choristers added their voices and very shortly the singing began to improve. Then, two years ago, the members of the choir, then numbering twenty-four, were placed together in seats near the organ at two sides of the room, and from that time the general singing began to be much better. Since then the choir numbers have increased to thirty, and it has been very encouraging to notice the development in musical taste and the greater facility in 'reading'. Attempts have been made with part singing: anthems, canticles and chants written in three or four parts are now regularly sung, and some of the famous versions such as Smart's Te Deum in F, and Stanford's Benedictus in B flat are also sung, thus familiarising the girls with good specimens of English church music. Nor has the lighter side of musical life been neglected and the choir has sung many glees and part songs. Dr Walford Davies' setting of Humpty Dumpty, a most humorous and clever piece of writing, was given one evening, and Debussy's setting of the 'Blessed Damosel' is soon to be presented.''

In 1910 the choir went to the Leeds Musical Festival to hear Dame Clara Butt sing, amongst other items, the 'Blessed Damosel'. Miss Davies writes ''The countenances of these aspiring young choristers presented anything but an encouraging spectacle as the last chords died away, while a deep gloom settled on everyone. It is a composition of most delicate beauty and charm, and music of its kind is very difficult, both to interpret and perform. At the rehearsals in the early stages the work was regarded with positive dislike, but as time went on the choir grew to appreciate it and made brave efforts to conquer the difficulties.'' At this time it is noted that badges were first presented to selected members of the choir, and the possessors evidently showed great pride in these marks of distinction.

As the years passed it is obvious that the emphasis on music and especially choral singing was of exceptional interest in the school, fostered by the knowledge and taste of Miss Davies. Form choral competitions were reported every year, often in an amusing but also critical way. Several adjudicators mentioned with appreciation the selection of the songs chosen for these competitions, and the list of works accomplished by the choir, year after year, is very impressive. It is obvious that in Miss Davies the school had an exceptionally talented and musical director and the girls were learning the very best of both classical and modern works. Such a foundation produced first class musicians as the years went on, and gave the School a high reputation in this field. When the chapel was built in 1923 Miss Davies was then an accomplished organist and composer, and music in the chapel was one of the chief interests in the College.

The first choral competition in 1911 is reported fully, when a silver cup was competed for by the forms. Some of the tests were unusual, including unseen sentences chosen by Miss Gask and intoned on one note as a test for clear articulation, while a further test was to monotone for pitch by counting slowly up to twelve on a fairly high note. The choral competition always ended with a song from the choir and the school songs sung by all. Later, when the competition was the annual event in every spring term, to produce it became a great test of the ability and organising powers of the house conductor.

Mention of the school songs, printed later in this book, calls to mind the emblems and mottoes, as these form subjects for the songs. The clover was the chief emblem and an account of the original clover brooch which was found by Miss Jones on a country walk has already been given. In 1912 at an Old Girls' Union meeting small clover buttonholes were presented to each girl, and Miss Jones spoke of the clover and its threefold meaning of industry, sweetness and strength, explaining that it also corresponded with the second school motto *Industria, Fide, Pietate*. She saw in the trefoil leaf a delicate complement to her Irish nationality and she liked to think of the girls in the past linked with those of the present and future. The clover was embroidered on all the "best" dresses, as well as on collars and cuffs, and even on the green pinafores worn in the evening in the school room, but embroidery became too expensive in later years and it had to disappear about 1930.

The Savery Bird was an emblem of the original boys' school and perpetuated on the badges and the hat band of the girls' school and above the school crest to this day. The actual bird is rather obscure but appears to represent an avocet species. On account of this emblem and its duck-like appearance the boys of the first school were referred to as the "Savery ducks". Some years ago when part of the building which had been the boys' school in Ripon Road was being demolished, a stone replica of this emblem was found and given to the bursar of the College for safe keeping.

The school crest contains the arms of Ripon, York, Knaresborough and Harrogate, with the motto *Industria, Fide, Pietate*. The other motto, chosen by Miss Jones, *Per Ardua ad Alta* is painted above the stage in the hall. Lord Davidson, Chancellor of the Duchy of Lancaster, and for many years chairman of the governors, gave the big doors into the old lecture hall opposite the front door and it is his crest that is also displayed on that door.

In these early days the literary and dramatic work of the College was very flourishing under two pioneers of special note. Miss Gask who was appointed in the first year of the new building had a great love of literature and the classics, and Miss Lena Jones who had joined her sister about the same time used her talents as an actress in many productions of note. The first performance, in 1904, was of *As you like it* and it was fully reported in the *Harrogate Advertiser* by Mr W H Breare. The introductory sentences are very graphic: "On entering the beautiful new buildings of the Ladies' College the stranger traversed the spacious corridors to reach the gymnasium (now the hall) and this apartment could hardly be recognised under its tasteful transformation. Soft electric lights and deep-toned drapery imparted a subdued but comfortable air to the auditorium, which, with its proscenium of curtaining, presented none of the tawdry effects of a theatre. The comfortable stalls and chairs were filled with a fashionable audience who, under the dim lights, seemed to add to the softness of the vignetted scene. As the curtain parted a bright woodland scene was disclosed and the play began . . . . The young ladies were word perfect and well rehearsed and not a palpable hitch occurred throughout the evening. Of course one must take into consideration the educational advantages those young people possess. The students are taught to speak the King's English clearly and distinctly. Also in deportment the girls walked on easily, gracefully and with that naturalness which is associated with birth and breeding." There follows a description of the parts played by the actresses, including Josephine Talbot, who played Audrey with delightful comedy, and Miss Lena Jones who was wholly admirable in her part as Phoebe. "To Miss Lena great praise is due for the clever way in which the pupils have been rehearsed. Miss Davies accompanied the songs and played incidental music with excellent taste. The object of the performance, the Yorkshire Home for Incurables, benefits considerably from this highly meritorious production."

The next play of note is *Le Bourgeois Gentilhomme* in 1908, again reported fully in the local papers. "The clever students of the Ladies' College have done many charming plays in the cause of charity and in this one freshness and spontaneity added rare charm to a refined interpretation. Verily it is a valuable experience for young ladies on the threshold of life."

In 1909 the play *Hippolytus of Euripides* was produced, with Miss Lena Jones as Hippolytus, and this was the first of several Greek plays done at the College.

As well as helping in many local charities in which Miss Jones took a special interest, other causes are often mentioned. In 1904 there is an account of the Kotady mission school in Ceylon for which contributions were collected, and a few years later there is a letter from the principal of the school asking for £10 for new furniture and £3 for a school bell. She writes: "If you could meet the teacher trudging through the sandy lanes every morning telling the children to come to school, you would see what a help it would be, and it would also be so useful to know when our evangelistic meetings were ready to begin. You would be greatly taken with the many Mohammedan boys with their pretty tall woven silk caps on the back of their heads. They learn their scripture verses every day with the hope they will get a present at Christmas. I should be so thankful if you could send me a box of toys for them, and work bags, beads, tiny thimbles and needle books for the girls."

During 1909 a committee was first formed for managing the distribution of money collected each term on behalf of the various charities as it was thought that "the girls would then feel that the arrangements are in their own hands". Dr Barnardo's Homes and a protegé and various other causes then received a regular donation. During this year there is the first record of the visit of Mr Hind Smith, one of the most noted of Dr Barnardo's leaders whose enthusiasm and talks raised a great deal of money for the cause and whose knowledge of hundreds of schools made him an entertaining visitor.

The first mention of games and physical work is in 1900 when hockey was played on a field near Percy Lodge and cricket and tennis at the boys' school field near Clarence Drive. A few girls went swimming in the Starbeck baths

1906 Miss Jones, sister Lena and members of her staff

and many girls had bicycles, some with the new "free wheels". Tennis was played by nearly all girls and four clubs were started, each club going once a week to the College field, not the least enjoyable part of this being the drive through the town in cabs! Matches were played against the Harrogate Ladies, Clifton Boys' College, and the Wesleyan Ministers. In 1902 hockey was made compulsory and a hockey coach came four times in the term. Birdie Brailsford was captain and went that year to Madame Osterberg's College at Dartford. In 1904 the school moved to its new buildings and girls from then on were able to play on the College ground and no longer had to carry gear over muddy fields as at Percy Lodge. The school was divided into four Houses for matches. The day girls formed one House, the lowest corridor formed another called Centre House and the upper floor was divided into North and South Houses. In 1906 there were improvements to the College grounds. "The field is in particularly good condition after the draining and levelling operations which interfered so much with the hockey last season and was a very heavy expense. The playground too has been asphalted and tennis courts made for winter play. A further great improvement has been to surround the grounds on Duchy Road with a high wooden fence (still there) which protects us from the intrusion of workmen and boys who stood on the bank to watch our games and did great damage to our trees and hedges and caused us much annoyance in other ways." In 1908–10 hockey, cricket and tennis were captained by Gwen Wilkes and it was reported that she made an excellent captain and her high sense of duty had considerably raised the standard of the teams. Gwen later spent a year or two on the staff to coach games and also was secretary to the Old Girls' Union for some time. In 1911 lacrosse was started in the school and matches were played against Wycombe Abbey and St Leonards. It was soon noted that lacrosse was very popular, some girls liking it better than hockey.

The athletic sports in 1909 seem to be the first big event on the College field, where many visitors were entertained and a varied programme of sports took place. These were throwing the cricket ball, flat races, bicycle races and many amusing events; decorated cycles representing themes such as Music, Japan, the Union Jack, were much admired. "All the hundred and forty pupils took part, the whole of them being suitably and prettily attired. The programme opened with massed drill which was very effective." At the sports day the prizes all seem to have been presented by the parents and staff and must have been quite a display, as the prizes for twenty four competitions are listed, such as writing cases, silver purses, Longfellow's poems and several hat-pin stands. Mr Bagenal in presenting the prizes said that they had had a most enjoyable afternoon and the Duchy estate had reason to congratulate itself upon having Miss Jones and the Ladies' College in their midst: there was nothing more delightful than seeing young people enjoy themselves and indulge in the kind of exercise they had just seen: this was a new thing in a girl's life.

The Christmas party, from very early days, was a unique event, a mixture of ceremony, old customs, music and feasting. The party was held in the lecture hall when the girls, all in their best white dresses, entered to bow to Miss Jones, who received them from her stance under the big Christmas tree, the whole room very beautifully decorated and lit by shaded lights. Then followed the procession of dainties led by two tall candles, as the many maids (then about forty) in their grey uniform and frilled aprons carried in dishes of all types, and curtsied to Miss Jones. The head cook brought in a flaming Christmas pudding and finally the housemen carried in the peacock pie and the decorated boar's head, to the singing of the Boar's Head carol. Then came the wassail cup carol while the prefects passed round the silver cups for a loving cup amongst everyone, and after a moment we heard Miss Davies' carol *Hail Father Christmas* and the large bearded figure arrived on a sledge with a team of elves, fairies, black cats or reindeer according to the whim of the producer. No-one knew his identity beforehand. "Who is he?" was whispered round. Some guessed the voice, sometimes he was an unknown friend of Miss Jones, generally very nervous, and often it was Dr Campbell Ward or Canon Guy of Christ Church. Later on members of staff were asked to take on this task, to make the speech and invent original ideas for giving out the presents from the sledge. Miss Jones was always given her beautiful book and there were rhymes or alphabet stories to guess and sometimes a little staff sketch. Then there was dancing, with a real band of four players, on the sprung dance floor of the hall, while Miss Jones and her guests sat in the "boxes" and looked down at the scene until supper time. It was an excited crowd even in olden days, but later, as the school grew, "the party" was some-

31

what of an anxiety to those who had to plan it. Supper in the dining room was a crowded feast with crackers and paper hats, and had to be in two relays, and finally all went back to the Christmas tree to sing a few carols and Auld Lang Syne.

When the School went to Swinton we did our best—and with a degree of success—to carry on the tradition. A lovely tree from the park filled the well of the main stairs and after supper the School collected on the steps and the two landings to sing carols, joined by Lady Swinton whose rooms were in that garden wing. When we came back to College the party proper was re-established. The assembly hall had by then become the North Dining Room, but the folding tables were carried away and the chairs stacked along the passage. Jean Radford's silver-framed paintings of carol stories and legends decorated the walls, and the Tree and Father Christmas were all there once more. There were our familiar guests, Dr and Mrs Campbell Ward, Dr and Mrs John Ward, the chaplain Mr Barker, and the bursar Mr Stone with their wives, the staff in their long dresses and the girls in their green silks: all joined in the fun and dancing, with Sir Roger at the end. In 1946 we started to move out on to the playground as a finale. Here under the stars we sang *Hark the Herald Angels* and then to *The First Nowell*, with hoods up, everyone walked into the darkened chapel, lit only by the sparkling white lights of the two altar Christmas trees. There were a few of the best known carols to be sung and finally Tennyson's "Ring out wild bells". The triumphant chorus "Ring out the old, ring in the new, Ring in the Christ that is to be" was something that stirred the spirit, and it was a quiet school that went away to bed to the sound of the choir's final processional music—"The holly and the ivy". As the years went on and young people's parties changed in style, so Father Christmas and the presents from the Christmas tree and the dancing disappeared in favour of a seasonal film. The Boar's Head and the wassail cup likewise were no more. Times change, but those who shared in the ceremonial of those early parties and the carol singing in the playground and in the Chapel will always remember the magical Christmas atmosphere that surrounded them.

As one reads the *Chronicles* of 1910–1914 leading up to the coming of age of the school, one is conscious that the first stage of the "building up" has been completed and a steady consolidation is taking place. There are references to buildings and houses being added, and Miss Jones was now watching closely as pieces of property near the school fell on the market. Clarence House, which had been a private dwelling, was equipped as a domestic arts (DA) house and the senior girls spent a year learning all branches of housecraft and needlework and the management of a home. The uniform was a pale green linen dress, with mob cap, apron and collar and cuffs, and a housewife's certificate was taken at the end of the course: the first teacher to organise the house was Miss Shaw. Behind Clarence was a block of coach house and cottage, and this became the original sanatorium. The next house, Woodlands Lodge, which had been a small school for boys, was added at the same time, and became the junior house for children up to the age of twelve. Miss Lena Jones was given the charge of this first preparatory department.

Claremont, across the road, was taken to provide a hostel for a few girls and Mrs Jones lived there during her later years. This house and its adjoining one, Armadale, later formed the boarding house of Armaclare. About 1913 the first part of Lincoln House, Highfield, was rented as an overflow for staff and girls, and shortly afterwards this, and the next house Lincoln Lodge, were bought, and then were joined together. Grove House, 18 Duchy Road, was bought for six staff, with its back garden providing two grass tennis courts: later it was sold, but re-bought in 1970 as a home for the headmistress. Rylstone and Penshurst, 13 and 15 Clarence Drive, used as waiting houses, soon also became school property.

Societies in the School, such as the Debating Society, the Art, the Camera Club, the Historical Society and particularly all aspects of games and music form the chief interests in the school magazines of this time. Old Girls who were to become notable for work at the university or in other spheres are remembered in detail, and one has a clear idea that with the headmistress in her most active years, helped by Miss Gask, Miss Davies and many ardent members of staff, the school had become a noted one throughout the country.

THE COMING OF AGE

The coming of age of the College, celebrated on 26 June 1914, was reported in the *Harrogate Advertiser*, and the following account is quoted to give a graphic description of the occasion:

"The Harrogate College was fortunate in the selection of the week-end for the coming of age and annual reunion of Old Girls, the weather being all that could be desired. About a thousand guests attended and the attractions included the finals of various races, the large and fashionable crowd deriving keen enjoyment from the sport. It was a brilliant assemblage flanking the school buildings, whose walls afforded a welcome shade from the hot rays of the sun. A feature of the afternoon's proceedings was the mass drill when all girls took part and executed a series of movements with the celerity and precision of an army of soldiers. Afternoon tea was served later, and the company gathered in the lecture hall where a full length portrait of the headmistress, painted by Mr Ernest Moore, an illuminated address and a diamond pendant were presented to Miss Jones by Dr Sibly, Mrs Savery's brother and president of the Private Schools' Association. Mr Servington Savery, brother of the founder, gave an address. During the evening there was a tournament of music, poesy, dancing and declamatory art. About two hundred and fifty girls were arrayed in fancy costume, and the scene, after the entrance of the procession, was very striking. The competitions had included poems on the coming of age, topical school ballads, amusing suffrage orations and others. The trophies awarded to the victors consisted of laurel wreaths and palm branches and produced an amusing sight with the Order of the Red Clover presented to the top competitor, Aileen Ellis. The celebrations ended with a special service held in the hall on Sunday when the Bishop of Knaresborough, in an inspired address, spoke on 'Influence, conscious and unconscious'."

C

It may serve to amplify this account of the coming of age and subsequent years, to give an extract from a later *Chronicle* written by Christian Robertson (Buist), a winner of one of the trophies, under the heading "Peace and War 1914–16".

"Casting my mind back I have a vision of my first summer term at Harrogate College when a great occasion was being celebrated—our school had attained her majority. The Muses must be invoked to sing her praises and we had done. our youthful best to invoke them. Clad in voluminous folds of butter muslin liberally ornamented with a Greek 'key' pattern—unfortunately the only key I ever possessed to the classics—I remember viewing the assembled company from under a laurel wreath that had certainly not been 'made to measure': it tilted rakishly over one eye of a flushed, and I hope, moderately, triumphant countenance. There were other crowned heads and many palm branches that evening, I hasten to add, but my crowning glory remains unique, ever green in my mind.

"Was it only a day or two after that that the Archduke Ferdinand was murdered and such pageantry quickly faded from our minds as the grim possibility of war was explained to us. I have little detailed recollection of those days at school in the early months of the war. The situation was only dimly comprehended by us, living as we did in such a sheltered life of orderly routine."

For the coming of age a number of poems were written and amongst these a set of new school songs by a few authors, girls and staff. These were set to music by Miss Davies and were sung frequently, whenever the school or the Union gathered together. The three favourites are printed here. The first was written by Muriel Pennington, the school secretary, and later the HCU secretary for many years:

> *Per Ardua ad Alta* what words are these we hear
> *Per Ardua ad Alta* resounding loud and clear,
> From east and west the sound rings forth and north and south reply
> As HC girls in every clime take up the joyful cry.
>
> One and twenty years have passed, so swiftly time speeds on,
> Till now on England's role of fame our school a place has won.
> Her children scattered far and wide are working for her still,
> For her they'd give their best, their all, and with a right good will.
>
> *Per Ardua ad Alta*, thus, thus our school has taught
> 'Tis but by earnest effort that the finest things are wrought,
> Strive on then, till our College gains the topmost rung of fame,
> And all the world pays homage to its loved and honoured name.

Written by an unknown author:

> There's a place that is dear to the heart of us
> It is one that has come to be part of us
> It is there we have learned to run hard in the race
> Play fair in the field and look life in the face,

Oh girls but we'll strive for its honour and fame
And ever shall we thrill to the sound of its name.
    Then Hurrah, Hip Hurrah, HC
    We are proud of the name HC,
        Per Ardua ad Alta
    Three rousing cheers—HC

There's a work in the world to be done for it
There's a place in the world to be won for it
At the head of the lists it's to carry the prize
Ad Alta! ad Alta! To rise! To rise!
Up, up with it girls, unsullied its fame
And made the world thrill to the sound of its name.
    Then Hurrah, Hip Hurrah, HC etc.

Written by Miss Davies; the song which has survived to the present day:

Song of the Red Clover

Talk not of the queenly rose, nor the stately lily fair;
Take me where the Clover grows with its breath of the glad warm air,
Fragrance of the fields it brings, the meadows all aglow
And the bee its honey sweet distils where the Clover red doth grow.
Clover red! Clover red! haunt of the humble bee.
Sturdy and straight, emblem of strength, sweetness and industry
Every flower hath its hour, but the Clover can never die
For to each girl here is the Clover dear and we all know the reason why.

Talk not of the gay world's spell, heed not its noisy clamour;
We know of a life more sweet than fine false dreams and glamour.
Out beyond are the flowers that fade, delights that are quickly over,
For us then the gladsome joy and strength of the folk that dwell in Clover.
Clover red! Clover red! etc.

CHAPTER II

Miss Jones' Headship

1914–1935

PERSONALITIES AND HAPPENINGS

The first few years of this era in the history of the College are dominated by the first world war. The *Chronicles* are curtailed, and news in them is often of Old Girls' war work or sad notices of casualties among fathers or brothers. Christian Robertson (Buist) continuing her account of "Peace and War" writes: "We did what we could to help. There were interminable skeins of khaki wool knitted into socks and scarves, helmets, and mittens, and despatched to the Front. These war days bring to mind our efforts to help the Belgian refugees as there was a houseful of them at the bottom of Clarence Drive, but I cannot recall that we had much personal contact with them. First Aid and Home Nursing classes were interesting additions to the time table, and there were occasional tea parties when we entertained the convalescent soldiers from the local hospitals. A minor repercussion of the war was that Fraülein disappeared, and instead of routine German lessons conducted with a certain Teutonic rigidity we spent many delightful periods in Miss Lena Jones' drawing room or in any spot where we could forget the classroom, to glimpse beyond mere grammar, something of the real grandeur of Goethe and Schiller: it was not just German that we were taught by Miss Lena but the finest of literature, and I shall always be deeply grateful."

During these years there were few internal changes. A secretarial course and a gardening course were started, and a room was set aside for war work where girls and staff spent much of their free time making splints, swabs and other VAD needs. About this time an Old Girl, Daisy Petter (Vincent), offered a prize for the best essay to be competed for among the seniors. This was called the Vincent Petter Essay and was in memory of her son. The prize

36

was awarded each year and the winning names recorded on an oak board. The first winner was Lucy Kitchen for an essay on "Fashions". The competition ceased after about fifty years when the pressure of examinations made it difficult for the girls, and the connections of the school with Mrs Petter's family ended.

Mrs Jones, Miss Jones' mother, died in 1918. She had lived in Claremont (Armaclare) for many years and took the keenest interest in the girls and their hobbies, and all were very fond of this charming old lady. The choir sang at her funeral service at Harlow Hill where all the members of the Savery family and the Jones family have their graves.

Only a few additions to premises were possible at this time but two of these are notable: In 1916 the beautiful house Oakdale in Kent Road was leased as the Junior House, and forty children transferred there from Woodlands in charge of Miss Lena Jones, helped by Miss Gent and Matron Millen (Tron). Woodlands then became the sanatorium, and the cottage behind was vacated and used as classrooms. The last two houses in the Lincoln block were bought in 1915 and a large common room and a dining room were made in the basements. The fifty girls had all their meals in Lincoln with a resident cook and housekeeper, and the house formed a complete unit under Miss Forde. Part of the house was used as a French house where senior girls could live for a term or more, speaking exclusively French in charge of the resident staff.

Until about this time organisations for competitions and matches were all in forms, and the form mistresses must have had this side of the life very much to heart. There were no common rooms as we now have them, and the form rooms were the meeting places, the desk being the place for spare time pursuits as well as work. After Lincoln became a House, with Clarence for domestic arts already a close community, the girls in the main building became York and Lancaster according to the floor on which they slept. York I had the first floor, York II the top floor, and Lancaster in between, each with their own matron, and Miss Gask in charge of the whole number. In 1922 when Balliol, which had been a small girls' school, was bought, each house had its own housemistress. Miss Spencer Smith was the first housemistress of Balliol, Mrs Blayney (Miss Davies' sister) soon took Armaclare, and Miss Brown had Clarence. These three small houses were called "Combined", a name which persisted for many years. Thus from this time the closely knit House spirit became an integral part of the life of the School.

Societies in School were obviously active and were much enjoyed. The Photographic Club produced many excellent pictures of interiors of the buildings and these provide much information of early days. Groups of girls and portraits were shown and a competition was held each year. The Art Club submitted pictures and drawings for an exhibition each summer. One of the well-remembered teachers was Miss Peppercorn who was very accomplished herself and produced beautiful pastel and watercolour sketches of such scenes as the bluebell woods at Ripley. Many people may still possess one of these delightful pictures which were often for sale in aid of the charities. The Historical Society's activities are described as discussing both historical and modern topics such as Ireland and women's suffrage: expeditions to the

c

monasteries of Yorkshire and the nearby churches to study the types of architecture were often planned. The Debating Society appears to have been very active, usually attended by about sixty girls, and the debates are fully reported. One, it is interesting to note, was on a subject "A Channel Tunnel would be advantageous to England" defeated by thirty-two to twenty votes. The Dramatic Society produced a great variety of plays and pageants. Miss Lena Jones was a fine actress and an enthusiastic producer, and a succession of drama mistresses gave the College a stimulating interest in this field.

In the 1919 *Chronicle* we read of the formation of a Guide Company. Previous attempts had evidently been made to establish the Movement, but now, under Miss Young and Miss de Vesian, and with Margaret Storey as Lieutenant, the 5th Harrogate Company was formed. From the accounts which from that time on appear in the *Chronicle* every year it is obvious that Guiding became a flourishing and popular activity, playing an important part in the life of the School. There were Brownies and junior Guides at Oakdale and more senior Guides at College, and the record of their successes, the Gold Cords and Badges won, and the interests pursued, makes impressive reading. In 1922 Miss Coutts (Mrs Blad) became Captain, with Miss Millar and Miss Thomas in charge at Oakdale. A room in the basement of the old sanatorium was fitted up as Guide Room. In 1926 Maud Coey, who was a young cousin of the Jones family and who had left College a few years earlier, took over the captaincy, an office which she held with notable success. She was supported by a number of skilled and enterprising Lieutenants, among them Marjorie Bain, Marjory Stratton, Joyce Banbury and Joyce Carter, and there are enthusiastic accounts of adventure trails, hikes, and above all the camping holidays which were held every year in a variety of locations, including especially pleasurably at Bewerley. For several years Miss Jones rented a house at Bewerley on the outskirts of Pateley Bridge, and the Guides were always welcome visitors there, where the grounds supplied wonderful camping facilities. We read that in 1933 Adza Hodgins was awarded the Guides' Silver Cross for Gallantry for her part in a drowning rescue, and in 1937 Maureen Bower was selected for the great honour of being the girl chosen to represent Great Britain, along with 19 other Guides from all over the world each representing their own country, at the Silver Jubilee Celebrations of the American Guides, held in New York. During the war years at Swinton Cadets, Rangers and Guides flourished busily, linking with the Masham Company in the various kinds of war work that were undertaken. In 1943 Miss Bacon, a Guider of experience who later became District Commissioner, took over the Company. In the post-war years, back in Harrogate, new interests claimed attention, and enthusiasm in Guiding gradually waned. There was a revival in the 60's under Miss Gaskell, and two successful camps were held, but with her departure the numbers again dropped, and the College Company finally disbanded, those who wished to do so joining up with local Harrogate Companies.

As far back as 1912 there are references in the *Chronicles* to groups of enthusiastic horseriders, but it was from 1922 up to the outbreak of war that riding really developed as a special feature of the College curriculum, and this was largely due to the Riding School run at that time by Mr Paisley and his wife. The land behind Oakdale was laid out as a riding field with a ring and jumps to provide training facilities, and from small beginnings the number increased to give the spectacular contingent of about 30–40 horses arriving on the front drive of College to set off in games time for hacks in the country, or to the field. Miss Brown took over the charge of the riding for a number of years and as a result of her keenness and her personal example, added to Mr Paisley's training, some very proficient horsewomen were produced from both College and Oakdale. A Gymkhana was arranged on the Oakdale field each year and this made a pleasant social occasion for parents and friends for a summer's afternoon. There was always an interesting display of riding skills to be followed by the presentation of a number of fine cups, variously given by Mr Paisley, Eileen Major, and others, for different aspects of horsemanship. Some girls were allowed to have day's outings to Fewston or to the local Hunts, and a number had their own horses in the stables. Miss Adams, who was a very experienced rider, gave help for a few years, and later Ursula Wales (Aitken) who had returned as a member of staff, was in charge. On the return to Harrogate after the war nothing could be done for several years. Small riding schools re-started but often changed hands, and it was only from about 1960 that we were able once again to include riding as one of the school's more specialised activities.

In 1922 a scheme of work attempted in various schools, called the Dalton plan, was started for all forms except the youngest girls. This was a system of free study and work assignments which originated in America, and an educationalist from USA came to College to help for a short time. Only an introductory lesson in a subject was given each week and girls had then to study on their own and consult the teachers for help as required. A complex system of cards used for recording assignments and progress were provided for each girl. This scheme suited the clever student, and also (in other ways) the idle student, but after two terms of strenuous efforts and much repetitive work on the part of the staff, it was found that progress in most subjects and for most of the girls was not as had been hoped, so the school returned to its normal timetable.

Each generation, both staff and girls, has its part to play in a school's history, some of the personalities making notable contributions. I, in my years at College, must have helped to greet and say goodbye to hundreds of teachers, watching also something like fifteen hundred girls come and go, and I am aware of how many there are worthy of mention in this book had space allowed. In this post-war period (my early years on the staff) there were some whom I particularly recall, either because of their outstanding influence, or because of later associations with the School. Miss Curry was head of the English department and started the Clover leaflet for original writing: later she became headmistress of Aigburth Vale High School in Liverpool. Miss Millar and Miss Thomas were at Oakdale in 1924, where they both stayed for thirty-four years, beloved by all the children. Miss Crowdy produced outstanding drama, *Alcestis*, *The Pageant of Famous Women*, and many plays of Shakespeare. There was Miss Hodgson Smith inspiring the history; Miss

Lainé teaching biology and Miss Bickerdike mathematics, both later to become housemistresses. Miss Brown in Clarence House, and later in Lincoln, is remembered by hundreds of her housewives from those times; Miss Sankey came in 1922 and stayed for forty-four years, ardent with her cane work and other crafts. Miss Millen, the petite but powerful custodian of the Music Corridors came for one term and stayed for over fifty years. Mary Auty (Kingswell) made her mark for prowess on the lacrosse field and as one of the early Heads of Choir in the Chapel: she was later secretary of the Union for several years and an HCU governor. She still keeps in close touch with College through her daughter Josephine now the current HCU governor. Marjorie Morgan (Bartram) played lacrosse for England and spent a year or two on the staff, partly as games coach: she too represented the Union on the Governing Body and her association with the School lasted until her death, with her two girls and also her son's four daughters as pupils. Isabel Herdman (Crawford) followed her sisters Kate and Ellice, both heads of school. Isabel sent her four daughters to York House and also had five nieces at College. She herself was HCU chairman and a Governor for eighteen years. There was Sybil Toler (Murray), head of school for two years. She has been for most of her life associated with College, first as pupil, then teacher of the juniors, a parent, Chairman of the HCU, later a school governor and finally, for ten

An early view of the School Chapel. The five embroidered Saints can be seen in the altar panels

years, as Chairman of the Governing Body, in which capacity she is further mentioned as this record continues. Anne Batchelor came to Balliol in its opening year, and after leaving took over the Scottish branch of the Union, using all her energies and organising power to make a wonderful success of this large scattered branch with its numerous reunions of enthusiastic members: she only gave up the branch recently after forty-four years. Another who was at School a little later was Rona McColl (Brown) who took an outstanding degree in law and whose legal knowledge was very valuable during her term of office as HCU Governor. Nancy Parkinson, one of my first sixth form science pupils, took her degree at London University and became a most distinguished member of the HCU. She was awarded the CBE and before her death, which sadly occurred a few years ago, she was made a Dame Commander of the Order of St Michael and St George for her work on the British Council and Service Overseas, the first woman, other than the Queen, to receive this distinction.

It is very evident that both staff and girls were inspired by Miss Jones' enthusiasm for the School and were proud of its growing development. The major project under consideration in the early post war years was the building of the chapel and this particular subject is of such importance as to warrant a separate section.

THE SCHOOL CHAPEL

The existing arrangement for Sunday worship was that the girls walked across the Stray to Christ Church for the morning service, the vicar of that parish being chaplain to the College, and in addition to this some services were held in the assembly hall. Miss Jones, with her keen concern for the spiritual influence in the School, was very much aware of the limitations of this arrangement and determined to improve matters. There had already, before the war, been the suggestion of building a chapel, the site proposed being the front lawn facing Clarence Drive. The financial target set was £3 000, a sum which does not seem so inadequate when it is remembered that the annual salary of a graduate member of staff at that time was about £100. Gifts had begun to come in from parents and well-wishers from 1914 onwards, and by 1916 the fund had reached £1 000. All active building schemes had been stopped by the war, and it was with despair that Miss Jones now realised that, with post-war conditions, a stone building of the type she had envisaged was far beyond the funds which could be raised. The *Chronicle* of 1918 tells of the prohibitive cost of building in stone and proposes as an alternative one that could be built "on brick foundations with a superstructure of asbestos or some similar suitable material". It would seem that the decision was taken to go ahead with this plan. The fund at this time stood at £2 900, and there followed a period of feverish activity and intense fund-raising pursuits to reach the target, now considerably above the original £3 000.

Miss Jones could not but have been disappointed at this lowering of her sights, since nothing but the best had ever been good enough for her school. It must have seemed as a gift from heaven when, in 1919, St Mary's Church, not far from the Valley Gardens, came up for sale. This small church, built of good Yorkshire stone, had been found to be unsafe in its foundations, and it had been decided to dispose of it and to erect a new church on a nearby site. When it came on the market Miss Jones seized the opportunity to buy it as it stood, the price agreed being £420! At that time she had insufficient funds to meet the cost of transferring the fabric and re-erecting it at College, and so by the terms of a supplementary agreement she was allowed to leave the stone on its site until 1923, provided that she assumed responsibility for any trespass or damage that might take place. St Mary's in the meantime built a new and larger church. It is because of this association with St Mary's that the College, after its return from Swinton in 1945, and until its numbers grew too large, held its annual Commemoration Service there, and that Oakdale regularly attended the church when not coming to the College chapel. Efforts to raise the additional funds were now redoubled, and at last, during 1921–2, the fabric was brought to the site on which the chapel now stands. There are photographs showing the huge pile of masonry heaped on that area. Work began on the foundations in October 1922, and the foundation stone was laid on 24 February, 1923. New stone pillars were needed and new roof slates, but the very good stone from St Mary's formed the main structure of the chapel. It may be of interest to people to know that the dark pine pews not needed in the chapel were for many years used as seats in the playground outside, and also, until quite recently, as the spectators' seats in the swimming bath!

A sizeable part of the 1922 *Chronicle* is devoted to one aspect or other of the chapel project. There is a photograph of old St Mary's and a sketch of what it will become when transformed into the College chapel. The building is described in some detail and much consideration is given to the organ which must be "a really good instrument". Regret is expressed that for the time being the budget will not stretch to include stained glass—"no doubt a matter for future generations". And finally we are reminded that "The chapel is to be a special memorial to the Founder, but let us always remember that the School as a whole is to be the memorial of his life and work".

As is to be expected, the chapel saga is continued in the 1923 *Chronicle*. The foundation stone ceremony on 24 February was complicated by badly adverse weather conditions, with indoor accommodation insufficient for the many visitors. The guests of honour were the Education Minister, the Rt Hon Edward Wood, and his wife Lady Dorothy. Most of the service was held in the School assembly hall, Major Wood, the clergy, the mayor of Harrogate, the headmistress and others braving the elements for the actual laying of the stone. We are told that during their absence the choir sang suitable music. There were speeches from Miss Jones, the Minister, and Mr Servington Savery, who was both Chairman of the Governors and brother of the Founder. It was obviously a day to be remembered in the College annals.

And now Miss Gask, Senior Mistress at the time, should be allowed to take up the story: "For the next six months we watched with such patience as we could muster the growth of the actual building as stone by stone it rose. Saturday September 29th, the Festival of St Michael and All Angels, was the date selected for the Dedication Ceremony. The few days previous to this date were full of anxiety as to whether the Building would be ready in time. Men were at work right through the nights of Thursday and Friday putting in seats and oak flooring. Actually the last nail was hammered in at 10.30 on the Opening Day. Charwomen hastily removed the last traces of dirt, and at 1.30 the doors were proudly thrown open to admit some of the earliest arrivals for the ceremony at 2.30. There was a great crowd and a very happy one. The labours and worries and disappointments of some years were forgotten in the joy of this golden afternoon—really golden in every sense: for the sun shone with the mellow splendour of a perfect September day.''

The Lord Bishop of Ripon performed the Ceremony and gave the address. The Choir sang "Non Nobis Domine" and the Service ended with the singing of the 150th Psalm and Handel's jubilant music "Let the bright Seraphim—". The enthusiastic support that was given to the whole Chapel project is evidenced by the number of individual gifts towards its furnishing. Among them we find listed the oak choir stalls given by the HCU to commemorate Miss Jones' 25 years of headship. Across the front is engraved in Latin an inscription which when translated reads: "To the greater glory of God, by whose will our beloved Head has already governed the School successfully for 25 years, the Society of Old Girls with grateful hearts have placed these Stalls—1923''. The altar was given by the school as a birthday present to Miss Jones. It is of carved oak with five arches, the spaces intended to be fitted with embroidery panels. On the advice of a consultant in church furnishings it was decided that there should be five women Saints worked on a blue silk background to fill these spaces, and a group of staff undertook the work, learning to do this intricate church needlework. The centre figure was St Ursula with her maidens, and the four others, each with her emblem, were St Cecilia, St Agnes, St Catherine and St Barbara. The panels were dedicated and put in position in 1926. There was however some difference of opinion about their suitability as an altar ornament, and they were temporarily replaced by plain brocade hangings and later by a very attractive simple blue and silver frontal designed by an aunt of mine in her school of Needlework in Bristol. This was so much liked that when, many years later, it had become worn out, an exact copy was worked for the College by the Sisters of the Convent at Horbury, and this still furnishes the altar. The Saints' embroidery panels were framed, and now hang in the alcove near the South door. The organ, a magnificent little instrument, was very largely the gift of Mrs Savery. The brass chapel bell had originally been afloat on the SS Emeliano Bilboa, but was destined from 1923 onwards to ring out daily in Clarence Drive during term-time summoning the School to its Morning Prayers. The oak lectern carved by Thompson of Kilburn was given later in 1938 by the parents of Lorna Macleod who was head of school at that time.

The final cost was found to reach the forbidding total of £15 506, considerably in excess of what had been anticipated. There were other sales of work, and eventually at Miss Jones' Birthday Party in October 1925, the school made the splendid gesture of presenting her with a cheque for the final £168 required to clear the debt. It gave her a wonderful birthday.

CHANGES IN CONSTITUTION.
MISS JONES' RETIREMENT

The completion of the chapel in 1923, after all the effort and planning that had preceded it, made that year a landmark in the School's history. Ambition did not, needless to say, stop there and, as will be seen in due course, there was to be further expansion and development to follow.

There was, however, another matter that had been exercising Miss Jones' mind at this time. With the war over and a more settled situation in prospect for the country, her thoughts turned, not unnaturally, to plans for the long term future of the school. By the terms of Mr Savery's will Miss Jones had been permitted to acquire a financial interest in the School, and by the end of the war she did, in fact, own one half of the capital, the other half being in the shared possession of Mr Savery's widow and of his brother, Servington Savery. Thus the College, a private school, was in the somewhat precarious position of being owned by three people, two of whom were over seventy. It was by now, from small beginnings, a flourishing concern of over 300 pupils, so that steps had obviously to be taken to ensure its future.

To pursue the story further we now have to leave Harrogate and go, rather surprisingly, to the small village of Monkton Combe in Somerset, where there lived as vicar the Rev Percy Warrington. When Mr Warrington died in 1961 he had been the incumbent at Monkton Combe for forty-three years, but his claim to fame lies not in that achievement, but in the fact that he at one time had control of educational concerns easily passing the million mark in value. Mr Warrington, although circumspect when necessary in expressing his views, was an ardent low church Evangelical, to whom anything that even faintly savoured of Anglo-Catholicism was suspect. He viewed with alarm the current trend towards high churchmanship, and it became his single-minded life's ambition to save the country from what to him seemed the danger of popery, and to convert it to the low church doctrine in which he so passionately believed. We do not know quite when Mr Warrington formulated his "grand design" but it must have been some time during the war years that he decided on two ways of furthering his objective. One was to work through the medium of the schools, thereby influencing the young people who would become the next generation. The other was to acquire the advowsons (livings) of as many parishes as possible so that he could control the choice of clergy throughout the country.

It was in 1921, when Mr Warrington was in his early thirties, that he went into action. He first purchased a school in Shropshire, known at that time as Wellington School, privately owned by the principal, Mr (later Sir John) Bayley, who had founded it in 1880 and who now wished to retire. A Board of Governors was formed with Lord Gisborough as chairman, and the school was renamed Wrekin College. A year later Mr Warrington acquired Stowe House in Buckinghamshire, the former residence of the Dukes of Buckingham and Chandos, and in 1923 Stowe School was founded. Mr Warrington had by now discovered that it was comparatively easy to borrow money for the

1924 Some of the first Governors. Rev P Warrington, Miss Lena Jones, Sir Cyril
Norwood, Lord Gisborough, Mrs Leitch, Miss Jones, Lady Norwood.

purchase of premises for conversion into a school provided only that its annual
income (from fees) would cover the interest rates of the loan, together with
enough to meet the gradual paying off of the mortgages over an agreed time
range. He also bought Canford, Lord Wimborne's house in Dorset, to be
opened in 1923, and the following year, 1924, he evidently turned his attention
to girls' schools. History does not record how he first met Miss Jones, but it
was just at this time that she was considering the future of Harrogate College.
Mr Warrington evidently realised the School's potential, and Miss Jones, on
her side, seems to have had sufficient confidence in Mr Warrington's aims and
ideals to feel that she would be placing the School in good hands. Before long
the transaction was completed and Harrogate College became part of Percy
Warrington's empire. Shortly afterwards he acquired Lowther College in N
Wales, and in 1926 he bought Sir George Holford's mansion in the village of
Weston Birt and Westonbirt School came into being. This was followed by
Felixstowe College and one or two others, and before long the total of Mr
Warrington's schools passed the dozen mark. His general plan was to
interfere little with the policies of the schools beyond ensuring that a sturdy
type of evangelical protestantism was taught, by a chaplain whose sympathies
were compatible with this doctrine. Every so often this uncompromising
attitude was bound to produce confrontation, at times minor and ridiculous,
frequently much more serious, and numerous stories are told of problems that
had to be resolved. It is unlikely that Harrogate College would cause him
much trouble on this account since Miss Jones' sympathies were towards

Methodism and far removed from any suspicion of the Anglo-Catholicism which he so disliked.

Now we can leave Mr Warrington for a while and return specifically to Harrogate College. In January 1924 Mrs Savery died suddenly, greatly mourned by Miss Jones and indeed by all who had known her. In June of the same year the School became a public school with a board of governors, the same, to all intents and purposes as that which was controlling all the other schools of the Group, but with the addition of Servington Savery. Lord Gisborough was the chairman and Sir Charles King Harman vice-chairman. Miss Jones was asked to continue as headmistress, and this she did, now in a salaried capacity, until her retirement ten years later.

A copy exists of Miss Jones' report given at the first meeting of the new school council in July 1924, and it remains a striking testimony to her life's work. In her introductory remarks, after welcoming the new board of governors, she says: "I look back on a long road of twenty-six years' travel with deep gratitude for a past 'profuse of blessing every side' and forward on our yet untrodden path with boundless confidence in the future. To doubt our future would be impossible: it would be treason to the past." She then offers a brief retrospect "on this significant day of our history", and there follows a superbly comprehensive summary of every aspect of the school and its organisation, achievements, and many activities. "Accommodation taxed to its utmost capacity—322 girls, 48 resident mistresses and 49 servants" is worthy of note! Reference to the HCU includes "There is a strong link between the past and the present in our Union of Old Girls. There are at present 514 life members besides a great number of occasional members." The concluding paragraph of her report should be given in full, so entirely typical is it both of the person and of the age:

1924 The second gymnasium with classrooms and study bedrooms above

"It has been suggested that I should include in this report a statement with regard to the educational aims and ideals on which the school has been built. Plato's vision of perfect education as of 'many a wholesome breeze blowing over pleasant places and blessing our youth with Truth, and Purity, mother of Truth', seems to be full of inspiration today for those engaged in such work as ours. In conclusion I should like to quote a sentence from the last address I heard our honoured founder give in public: 'We must remember that the whole of human nature and the child should be so trained as to enter fully into the glorious heritage of life, with all its possibilities'."

Mr Warrington had every reason to congratulate himself on the Harrogate acquisition, and particularly on the fact that Miss Jones was to remain on as headmistress, thus ensuring stability over the transition period. She had outlined her plans for future expansion and development, indicating clearly the improvements and additions required, and the governors in their turn expressed approval and appreciation of the ambitious programme, and gave assurance of their ready support, financial and otherwise.

The records of the next few years are those of a flourishing school, obviously held in high repute. In 1925 we read of a "fine scheme" in progress—"the building of a new gymnasium, with three large class rooms over it, capable of being converted by means of specially constructed moveable partitions into a large junior hall, the addition of extra bedrooms, bathrooms and music rooms in this wing and a cloakroom to use as a green room under the new gymnasium stage. This scheme completed the new wing, begun many years earlier with so much foresight." Improvements were also going ahead in the boarding houses which at that time, and indeed until the return from the war years at Swinton, each had their own dining rooms and catering arrangements. Electric light, we are told, was installed in the part of Lincoln that was lit by gas. The school received a gift of a wireless set and so was able to listen to 'some excellent speeches and concerts'. There was an HMI Inspection which seems to have come and gone as do most school Inspections. In June 1927 Britain had the unusual experience of a total eclipse of the sun which moreover was visible in Yorkshire, and on such a special occasion the opportunity had to be seized for all the girls to see this phenomenon. The line went through Richmond and Leyburn about thirty miles from Harrogate in the Dales, and it was due at 7.30 in the morning. Accordingly, all the school was roused about 3 am for breakfast and then set off in twelve buses with rugs and picnics to join the continuous cavalcade of cars and coaches up the narrow country lanes. A place had been 'booked' on a hillside, 'lats' had been dug the day before under the supervision of Maud Coey, the Guide captain, and all settled down to await the sun rise. We saw the early sun partially obscured, with the darkness again shrouding the fields and woods, but then a cloud passed over, so that none of the eclipse proper was visible to us on that stance! However it was a very unusual picnic, and a sleepy school went to see Richmond Castle and Easby Abbey before going home to enjoy the unaccustomed luxury of an afternoon in bed.

Many photographs and sketches show stages in the evolution of the uniform, but on the whole it varied very little from decade to decade except in

47

detail. A notable addition in 1924 was the green cloak which had become necessary for crossing to Houses and going to the games fields: ever since its introduction this enveloping wind-shield has been a treasured garment long after school days had ended. The first photograph taken of the School going into Chapel shows the girls still attired in their panama hats and white serge coats and skirts (subsequently replaced by beige summer coats). In the post war years the thick woollen stockings, brown for the day time and black for the evenings, were discarded in favour of the strong lisle "bullet-proofs". A pleated tunic with velvet yoke was worn by all during school hours.

The first official outfitter was Mr Lebbon who had a small tailor's shop in Harrogate near the Pump Room. Here he, with one or two assistants, produced practically all the clothes that a girl required. Mr Lebbon's little premises was the meeting place of most new parents and their children, and he knew the name of nearly every girl, and often that of her mother before her. Girls were measured and tailored for their coats and skirts, overcoats (called Ulsters), tunics and all else. On Mr Lebbon's shelves were the green velour hats and the less important "squash" hats for every day. These latter small green felt hats became shrunk in the wet weather, assuming the shape of a jelly bag, stuck on the top of the head and frequently blowing off. In time these were replaced by green woollen caps, and the velours by berets with a coloured button to denote the house. Now, in this generation, hats have gone altogether, but the day may yet return when the comfort of a woollen cap for stormy days, so popular with all the young housewives of Harrogate, is recognised, and it comes back to favour.

Mr Lebbon stocked the blouses, the overalls, the underclothes, including Chilpruf combinations to sell to those mothers who thought they were necessary. Dark green knitted knickers were worn under all uniform, and these, designated "jocks", and the reseda Liberty dresses for afternoons, called "berties", completed the familiar inventory names.

As time went on, in line with the physical training colleges, a garment purporting to give more freedom in the gymnasium, was introduced. This was probably very carefully designed, but did not prove ideal, as it consisted of a short sleeved woollen pullover with long matching close fitting woven shorts reaching to the knee. Stockings were still worn and a gap ("a smile") was not allowed where garments joined. It is not surprising that the gymnasts became overheated, causing this innovation to be discarded: later many boxes of these excellent cover-up clothes found their way to institutions in Leeds and Bradford, and we sometimes wondered what the inmates made of them!

With the advent of the cotton tunic and aertex blouse, no stockings and baggy cotton knickers, things began to get better for gymnastics indoors, and for out of doors in summer, but the highlight of emancipation was reached when one mass drill display was concluded by "A" division doing its vaulting in knickers without the tunic. Miss Jacob had one or two letters from parents after that occasion, not quite sure that it was correct for their daughters to be thus displayed on the field.

Footwear until quite recently was, of course, entirely uniform, with strap slippers all day, brown in the morning and black after tea. Goloshes were a

1926 Chapel flower service with girls in their Sunday uniform

"must" for all girls and worn on every rainy day over the slippers to cross to chapel or the Houses. One of my early memories of Miss Gask is of her standing on the playground giving reproofs or order marks to those not wearing goloshes. Small things are remembered: after our removal to Swinton at the outbreak of war hundreds of things left behind in the summer holidays in cloakrooms, formrooms or cupboards, arrived in jumbled confusion at our new home, or never arrived at all. One York House mother wrote a very complaining letter that her daughter's goloshes had been so mislaid. I can still remember the girl's name.

The "best" dresses went through various stages, with the Liberty tussore for parties, followed by white dresses for everyone for special occasions, and then the green silks with clover leaves on the collars. These latter were very attractive dresses for a school, and there are many photographs of them on Speech Days.

Mr Lebbon had to come out of business when the clothing trade became difficult, but Forsyths of Edinburgh, who had for long been the suppliers for the many girls from Scotland, offered him whole time work. For his last few years he gave good service as the cutter of all the cloaks, which, unlike other parts of the uniform, were a very specialised item. One or two shops in Harrogate have at times taken over parts of the clothing with some success, but it is still Forsyths in Edinburgh who are responsible for the most important parts of our green uniform.

The *Chronicles* of 1926 and 1927 are largely full of domestic happenings—games, outings, concerts, debates, drama and even a pageant, all in full measure, and over it all the kindly, and when necessary formidable, presence of the headmistress who loved her school and everything appertaining to it.

1926 A botany ramble

1933 The swimming bath

In 1928 there comes the first official mention of a swimming bath "which had been longed for by so many generations of girls". The architect was to be Mr Taggart, Miss Jones' brother-in-law, who had so successfully dealt with the new wing extensions and with the chapel plans. The constructional details are given in the *Chronicle* with great precision, together with very attractive sketches of what the bath should look like. "A certain drainage difficulty affecting the conveyance of the water" meant that it had to be raised above ground level. All these problems could be overcome, and there remained only the question of cost. The estimated sum of £6 000 (later raised to £8 000) could not be met by the Council, but they did guarantee up to one half if the School could raise the rest. This was a challenge that had to be met, and once again everyone stirred themselves to see how it could be done. Enough money was forthcoming for the work to be begun without overmuch delay, and the official opening took place in May 1930. A bazaar to raise funds was planned to coincide with the Commemoration Week-end of July 1931, and the HCU Reunion was held at the same week-end. It was obviously an ambitious project, involving a year of preparation, and although the amount realised is not quoted, it would seem that the proceeds, together with gifts from other sources, were sufficient to complete payment of the bath. Credit must be given to the architect and others connected with the building for a first class piece of work on a difficult site. Through the years the College swimming bath was to prove a tremendous boon to the School, and the envy of many.

Miss Jones was now in the last years of her headship and had every reason to be proud of the flourishing public school which she would shortly be handing over to a successor. But all was not well. Since 1924, when Mr Warrington and his board of governors had assumed responsibility, Miss Jones had been a salaried employee and no longer in control of the school finances. The revenue from the fees went direct to the school company, which was controlled by the governing body who dealt with all money matters and settled all accounts. From her knowledge of the number of pupils and the regard with which the school was held, Miss Jones knew that it was more than paying its way and should be in a sound position financially. It was therefore a cause of great bewilderment and concern to her to receive complaints from the tradesmen that their bills were not being paid, and it cannot have been any comfort to learn that other schools in the Group were in the same predicament.

It is, perhaps not surprisingly, to the Rev Percy Warrington that we have to return for enlightenment as to what was happening. However doubtful the policy of using the revenue of one school to finance the mortgage of the next one might be morally, it seems to have been permissible in legal terms. Had Mr Warrington contented himself with this procedure there is no knowing how far it could have been continued, but it was a different matter when he extended his interest to concerns that did not give an annual revenue.

In his anxiety about what he considered to be the rising menace of Anglo-Catholicism Mr Warrington had turned his attention to the second part of his plan, which was to secure, by purchase, the patronage of as many livings as possible throughout the country. This, he figured, would give him the most effective means of influencing the selection of clergy. It proved to be a fruitful exercise from his point of view, but was one which was watched with growing unease by those not in agreement with his form of churchmanship. He was eventually halted by Act of Parliament, but not before he had obtained control of a great number of livings. It would seem that in this operation Mr Warrington's religious fervour was stronger than his business sense. His only source of revenue came from the fees obtained from his schools, and this he now diverted for the purchase of the advowsons of the livings, from which, of course, there was no resultant revenue. The finances of the entire organisation seem to have been so firmly under Mr Warrington's control that even the governors did not suspect what was happening. Before long there was no money to meet either the mortgages or the numerous school accounts. By 1933 the whole concern was so deeply in debt that the banks refused further credit and the schools found themselves unable to meet their expenses, including the day-to-day tradesmen's bills.

The insurance company most deeply involved was the Legal and General Assurance Association, and it was they who now took charge and assumed responsibility for rescuing the schools from the disaster which had engulfed them. Amongst their conditions of acceptance of this undertaking was the immediate resignation of Mr Warrington and his colleagues. A new organisation known as the "Allied Schools" was formed, and in 1934 Mr Kenneth Adams, a chartered accountant, was appointed as general secretary. Mr Adams was to devote his whole working life to the cause of the Allied Schools, and when he retired in 1965, he could look back on 30 years of dedicated service during which time he had, by his administrative skill, successfully steered the schools through all their vicissitudes, including their wartime tribulations. His interest was not confined to the financial side, although this, including the gradual paying off of the large mortgages, had to loom large. He was highly knowledgeable on all matters educational and exerted a positive and sensitive influence on the schools' progress. Each school was given the freedom to develop its own personality and had its own board of governors. Over and above there was the coordinating central committee on which were representatives from each of the individual governing bodies.

Dr (later Sir Cyril) Norwood became the first chairman of the central committee. He had been, amongst other things, headmaster of Harrow and president of St John's College, Oxford, and was one of the foremost educationalists of his day. At a time when they so badly needed help the Allied Schools could not have found two more able or dedicated men, and the debt owed to them is very great. It is neither possible nor necessary to dwell further on what had to be done before the complications that had been inherited could be considered solved. It took time and courage, but solved they were, and the Allied Schools group has long since taken its place in the forefront of independent education. Perhaps as an epitaph to Percy Warrington it should be said that, reprehensible as some of his doings were, he has to his credit the establishing of some very fine schools who owe their existence to him. The Allied Schools now comprise Stowe, Canford and Wrekin as boys' schools, Harrogate, Westonbirt, Felixstowe and Lowther on the girls' side, and one preparatory school Riddlesworth Hall. Not all of these were actually founded by Mr Warrington, but all had come under his control and because of this became associated as members of the Allied Schools group.

All this was happening during Miss Jones' last year at College. The new board of governors was announced at the commemoration week-end of 1934, when some of them were present. Although it was not publicly known at the time, this was to be Miss Jones' last speech day. A great era was coming to an end. No one tracing the School's progress from its unpretentious beginnings in the 1890s to the prominent position which it now held could fail to appreciate Miss Jones' total commitment to this pioneer work during her thirty-seven years of leadership. It does not require much imagination to understand the distress and agony of mind she must have suffered as she faced the possibility of the insolvency and even closure of the School to which she had dedicated so many years of her life. It was a happy decision to co-opt her on her retirement as a member of the governing body, thus ensuring that she would be kept in touch with events. She was always a welcome visitor to the School, and as years passed had the immense satisfaction of knowing that all was again well with College, and that her dreams for its future were being realised.

Miss Jones retired in April 1935 and a gathering of several hundred members of the Union came to the School to bid her farewell. At the meeting Miss Jones was presented with a cheque which she handed back to the Chairman to form an Entrance Scholarship for the daughters of Old Girls. In her speech of thanks she said that it gave her great pleasure to know that the girls wished

Miss Jones and her staff at the time of her retirement. In the front row can be seen Miss Bowen, Miss Spencer-Smith, Miss Gask, Miss Jones, Miss Forde, Miss Davies, Miss Brown, Miss Hewlett, Miss Bickerdike

d

to participate in her future home and purchase a lovely garden, but she would still have her garden, not so big and beautiful perhaps as had been desired for her, and it would always be her Old Girls' garden, associated with them and with their charming thought.

Many tributes have been paid to Miss Jones and in particular those written specially for the monograph on her ninetieth birthday, but on looking back it may be that for those who knew her at College, she is remembered in particular for her addresses to the School, ranging as they did on ethics, school problems, literature and poetry, and the spiritual and Christian principles she so firmly upheld: she was an outstanding speaker, with a clear compelling voice who gained attention in the first few words and held her listeners to the end. Miss Jones' "talks" were occasions for anticipation and always subsequent admiration. For other gatherings also, outside the School walls, she was a source of entertainment and interest in a small circle as well as on frequent public occasions. Her personal charm in many other ways remained undimmed to the end, so that those who knew her only in her later life could appreciate what she had meant to the girls for whom she had been headmistress. Now, twenty years after her death, it is interesting to trace what is known of the history of her life and to see from her many references to "Our Founder", that from the moment she came to Harrogate as a young untried headmistress, full of ideals, ambitions and boundless energy, she was always greatly influenced by Mr Savery's undoubted personality. But Miss Jones was no mere follower; she was a pioneer in her own right, and it is very evident that she was one of the notable and distinguished headmistresses in the sphere of education of her day.

Lady Bell (then Miss Lena Jones) retired with her sister after thirty-seven years at the school. Her contribution to the general life in the early years had been largely with drama, and she took leading parts in the plays and taught acting with great success. She was also a fluent speaker of German, and was the chief organiser, together with her brother, Mr Bertie Jones, of a special educational tour for English and American Schools to Germany and Oberammagau in 1934. Miss Lena had charge of the first junior house in Woodlands Lodge and then moved with the children to Oakdale in 1916. This lovely house and grounds was the setting of many parties, both for the children and Miss Lena's friends, parties that were always full of gaiety whenever Miss Lena held sway. With his sisters, Mr Bertie Jones, who had been bursar at the College for some years, also retired. His interest and energy had never faltered and he had a sincere appreciation of all matters connected with the school. Thus ended an era of family connections which had influenced the College for over forty years.

CHAPTER III

Miss Jacob's Headship

1935–1952

THE PRE-WAR YEARS AT HARROGATE

Miss Jacob came as headmistress in 1935 with a high reputation as a classical scholar of Girton and a triple blue in hockey, netball and tennis. It is difficult to reproduce from the *Chronicles* of 1935–39 extracts which give any adequate account of the progress during those years. Miss Jacob's reports of school life and interests on successive speech days make inspiring reading, telling as they do of many excellent examination successes and of prowess in games. There was much enterprise and vigour in all departments, particularly in dramatic work and music: art and science was going ahead with the promise of new premises in the near future. *Iphigenia* was one of the outstanding plays produced at this time and a particularly interesting summer speech day event in 1938 was an ambitious programme of Greek myths and dancing which is still remembered, not only for the unique production, which was the result of the efforts of everyone, staff and girls, but also for the colourful scene on the field with the moving processions of graceful dancers and athletes. In these four years before the outbreak of the second world war some additions were made to the Oakdale premises as the need for extra space had become urgent. A large extension, consisting of a new gymnasium, music rooms, dining room and a number of bedrooms was built, and during the same year the sanatorium at College was enlarged and modernised. Lord Davidson, Chancellor of the Duchy of Lancaster and later the chairman of the school governors, opened these new buildings in 1937.

Several well-known personalities retired during this time. Miss Gent who had been at Oakdale for twenty-five years left in 1935 as did Miss Violet Gask, member of staff and vice-principal since the School began in its present building. Writing of her, Miss Jones said: "Her name is a household word in all circles where the School is known. Her teaching powers and scholarship successfully stood many searching tests and her pupils widely recognised the value of what they received both at the time and even more in later years." Miss Gask ("Pipe" as she was affectionately called) was much loved by all who knew her, both in Lancaster House and throughout the whole community. Her place was taken by Miss Veitch from Cheltenham who worked hard for the College during the evacuation months but decided to seek other work soon after the arrival at Swinton. During these years too Muriel Pennington was obliged to relinquish her post as secretary of the Union which she had filled for seventeen years following her work as school secretary. In those days the secretary of the HCU combined all the tasks of the Union and during her last few years a directory of all the members was compiled and published. Writing of her, Miss Jacob said: "I have been able in my short time as the new president to realise something of the energy which she must have expended in the service of the Union and through it of the School as a whole'. Very sadly indeed, at a comparatively early age, Muriel Pennington died of polio, contracted from a little child she was nursing: her loss was a great grief to the hundreds who knew her.

Much could be written about the music which continued to flourish exceedingly under Miss Davies, sponsored by Miss Jacob, herself a good musician. Bach's St Matthew Passion which was performed annually in chapel every Easter, became one of the major events of the musical calendar, a tradition which was carried on by Miss Williams and later by Mr Pope. The entire school took part in the production, with visiting musicians taking the solo parts. It was always an impressive and moving event, unforgettable by those privileged to be present. Who, for instance, would ever in the future hear the stupendous "Crucify" chorus, or feel the awesome hush as the closing

1936 Start of outing to Bolton with Rita Turnbull the Head of School

1939 Mr Hinchley, cricket and lacrosse coach with some of the team which toured
Canada

notes died away into silence, without recalling those chapel performances?
There was also much Christmas Music, including Miss Davies' Christmas
Fantasy and many carols. Some of the girls presented a large radio gramophone to the School and records were played at evening assemblies and
recitals given to the Music Club on Sunday afternoons and in the evenings.
There was a great variety of programmes: Shakespeare as the inspiration of
the Musician, Beethoven the Jester, Parsifal, and others, and one is struck
once again by Miss Davies' knowledge and versatility and the wonderful
training in all branches of music that the girls were given even as she herself
began to reach the age of retirement.

At this time too the games of the College were outstanding. The lacrosse
team had its first "tour" and stayed in London to play Roedean, Benenden
and Putney Ladies, with Dorothy Openshaw as captain and Miss Preston in
charge. Mr Hinchley, a fine elderly coach, was invaluable on the lacrosse
pitches for many years. Miss Jacob played hockey for Yorkshire and hockey
was restarted at College and continued on a voluntary basis until some years
after the war. Rita Turnbull was head of the School in 1935 and played
lacrosse for England. Later, as Mrs Dolbey, she coached and selected for
many years afterwards. Now, as these notes are written, she is Mrs Marlow
and still a very important figure in the School as the present chairman of the
HCU. Tennis was not easy to organise as there were very few hard courts at

that time and the grass ones marked out in summer at the bottom of the field were not always in use because of wet weather. Arrangements were made for various forms to have tennis in lesson periods which gave each girl more practice. For the summer game cricket was played by all: fielding practices were conducted by the house captains every day at break and in spare moments, and there was much coaching in batting and bowling at the nets. Many of the girls became enthusiastic cricketers and there were frequent matches. A few special social occasions were highlights in the summer term, such as the match against the doctor's team or Mr Stott, the vicar of Beckwithshaw's team, and these, with those against the estate staff, and against the junior boys of Grosvenor House School, gave the opportunity for much fun and a big team tea. At matches the onlookers were all expected to score, and girls had their own score books and thus learnt the real points of the game. Swimming was a favourite summer sport and riding was very popular. One unusual feature of the physical work was the noted Morning Run. Everyone came to morning chapel wearing sweater and games shoes and the whole school walked away down Clarence Drive to the side entrance of the Valley Gardens to run a specified route round the paths and so back to College. This spectacle of three hundred or so girls running in the gardens was often of great interest to visitors who were staying in the nearby hotels and "taking the waters" for the "cure", in the early morning.

In 1938 preparations were being made to take the school cricket team to Canada in the following summer. A team from Roedean and one from a Newcastle school were also in the party, all sponsored by the Overseas Educational League. The teams were to play cricket in demonstration matches in various Canadian cities. The gathering clouds of war, during the summer term of 1939, had drifted away, and the sixteen College girls, with Muriel Spiers as captain, and Miss Jacob, Miss Preston and myself, left on the *Empress of Britain* on 5 August. Those who were privileged to go on this tour had a memorable experience. We were guests in private homes and sometimes in halls of residence of the universities. The Canadian hostesses were lavish in their hospitality and there were display matches at Montreal, Ottawa and several at Toronto. Visits were also made to summer camps and to Niagara. The renewed threat of war gathered momentum during the latter part of August and the organisers began to make plans for an early return. Miss Jacob and I had left for a week-end in New York to visit the World Fair when war was declared, and we hastily returned to Toronto to consult our official escorts to see what could be done. I still remember the enormous headings in red and black in the newspapers, telling of the outbreak of war, and have vivid memories of our great anxiety as to our journey home. Some of Harrogate College had finished school the previous July, but they, and all members of the team, were received as pupils in Branksome Hall School in Toronto until permission could be obtained from parents to allow them to travel by sea: most of them returned in November of that year. Miss Read, the headmistress, gave every possible help to our girls, including supplying them with much needed winter clothing. A new building at Branksome Hall was named Harrogate House in commemoration of the sojourn at the school.

1940-46 Swinton Hall

THE WAR YEARS AT SWINTON

The School had been told some months previously that in the event of an emergency the Harrogate premises would be commandeered, and had been asked to make provisional plans for evacuation. In England therefore, Miss Jones, who was asked back to help, Miss Davies, and the governors had completed the arrangements for the "Move" to Lord Swinton's home. Miss Jacob and I and the other staff arrived back in ships' convoy, after a three weeks' voyage, towards the end of September, and until we docked (in deep blackout) we did not know whether the School would have already moved. We made the night journey to Harrogate, collected our dogs, and then drove the twenty miles to Swinton Hall where the girls were arriving next evening for the opening of term.

It was on 3 September that war was declared, and at Harrogate, within a few days, a convoy of furniture vans had been requisitioned, and with the help of an army of unemployed labourers everything was taken from the school and transported to Swinton. When we look at the desks, beds, wardrobes, laboratory furniture, library books and everything else, now so neatly housed and placed, it seems impossible that the tremendous upheaval could ever have been accomplished. There were all the book bundles, the office records, the personal possessions of many resident staff, the crockery and kitchen utensils, the bedding and the dispensary cupboards, and these were all carried to Masham in about three weeks. Lord Swinton moved out most of his precious furniture and we moved in our more mundane possessions. What would not go inside the hall was ranged in marquees on the cricket pitch. Some time later there was an auction sale of Harrogate College "surplus". It was indeed an opportunity for the residents of Masham to gather something "going for a song". Beds and chests found a place in some homes in the village which hearsay related had been bought for 1/- a piece. It was difficult during the first few months at Swinton. Girls slept ten or twelve in a room and more in the long picture galleries. There were only five bathrooms to begin with and hardly more basins except for the jug and ewer variety. Bath lists were made out as usual, except that a teacher had to accept an excuse for missing a lesson because that period was assigned to some girls for their bath. I well remember that after about three weeks we *had* to do something so that hairwashing could begin, and we bought up all the village stock of enamel bowls and cans for this purpose. Cooking for the school was a major problem as the only ovens were heated by coal which had to be put on the stoves by the bucketful continually. There was no gas until calor gas was later installed. Belle, the cook, came with us from Harrogate, but few knew how she performed the miracles in that kitchen.

As the war continued the catering was often very complicated and Miss Brown did a magnificent piece of work when she took over both catering and housekeeping. It is extraordinary now to recollect that for most of those years each girl had her labelled pot of jam on the table which had to last a month; that bread, meat and butter were rationed (although the Masham tradespeople were very good to us) and that we had to eat what the government authorities sent us, or not eat at all. On one occasion we were issued with hundreds of cases of pilchards and had to have pilchards à la mode for day after day. There was nothing but a private supply of electricity, and everyone had to go to bed at 8 pm on a winter evening when the electric motor and batteries faded out. There was no large hall in which to assemble, so it was a contrivance to have prayers, lectures and dramatic performances in an entrance hall which we should have thought would suffice for eighty, whereas two hundred had to get into it. We used to reckon that each girl could secure about one square foot of floor space on which to sit if she could manage to dispose of her legs somewhere else. A flight of steps went out of the hall, and to have a piece of the stair was the luxury you grew up to when you attained the sixth form. Despite the cramped quarters, it is wonderful to notice, when one reads the old *Chronicles* of all we managed to do and produce in that room. Remarkably entertaining plays, concerts, and variety entertainments were put on with no scenery but the window curtains and perhaps a screen, and Sunday after Sunday we had our evening service there, since it was too far and too dark to go down the long country road to Masham Church.

As the first year passed we began to adapt ourselves to our new surroundings. The new class room block which had been promised could not be built because of war-time restrictions, and up to the end of our stay we had to have two forms in each room, one end having a lesson and the other end doing "prep". Lady Swinton kept a small wing for herself and her family and often could be seen looking over her stairhead at UIV[3] in the well beneath. For some time art was done in the conservatory among the camelias and ferns with the drips from the morning watering: the squash court, with one horse as apparatus, was the gymnasium. After a few months we turned the stable stalls into bathrooms and showers which were reached by a little dark tunnel built across the stable yard. A large granary provided a dormitory for twenty Lincoln girls with all corners of the outbuildings utilised in every ingenious way. The garage made a very good laboratory with the hose for a water supply and methylated spirit lamps for Bunsen burners until Calor gas could be introduced. We were warm in that good garage, but the biology classes had only the closed-in wash down, and were not so comfortable. The domestic classes had to be much reduced in number as the harness room was their quarters with the only fire the little grate in the corner, used by the coachman in former days. Later electricity was introduced, but Miss Brown "managed" there as she always could, amongst the smell of leather and polish, and with the help of Nick, her Scottie, who sometimes caught a stray rat when it appeared under the door. One of the most successful adaptations was the "Music Corridor". For many months the pianos were housed in bedrooms whither all girls went for lessons and practice: great was the relief when we secured the "lease" of Lord Swinton's row of brick-built dog kennels, used in the days of peace for his shooting parties' dogs. Each kennel just held a piano and the sound of music was at last taken out of ear shot. The grid eventually provided us with more electricity for cooking, lighting and a little heating: we managed to supply one hook somewhere in the passages for every girl to hang her cloak, and the Long Corridor was furnished with sofas and chairs from various houses at College to become the general common room for all the seniors after supper.

During the first winter the staff had found rooms in the village and walked or bicycled the two miles or so to school, but after a time we were able to rent the Glebe House in the meadows behind the church to make a comfortable staff residence for about a dozen teachers. Some of the staff did not enjoy their nightly walk home when eerie shapes of friendly cows loomed beside them, and the blackout was an affair closely controlled by the village policeman. A large fine was extracted from Miss Williams for one incident. Her first bedroom was in the King's Head in the Square, and she had forgotten to draw the black-out in her excitement over a forthcoming concert: mystified spectators could see a lady, standing on her bed, practising conducting with vigour, presumably for her bedroom companion with her violin.

At the beginning of the war few parents could visit their daughters, but as time went on a little petrol could sometimes be saved for the journey, and then the parents would beg a spare bedroom from a Masham householder and arrive with stores and picnics to stay the night. Firm friends were sometimes made in this way. Sybil Murray, our later chairman, occasionally visited her daughter Anne and spent her week-ends in a cottage on the estate belonging to Mr Jackson the shepherd. In the first two winters the frost was particularly severe. The water froze in the pipes under the ground and some of the needful supply had to be carried from a pump. The home lake froze thickly so it was possible to skate just outside the front door. One evening Lady Swinton had a party and invited many girls with her visitors and it was a unique sight to see the skaters in the moonlight practising their art and eating the hot potatoes which a squad of helpers were roasting on the wood fire on the bank.

We lived amidst magnificent pictures—Gainsboroughs, Romneys, Reynolds, Ibbotsons and many others. The sixth form had Lord Swinton's library as their form room, although his collection of books occupied all the large cases: they had to make visits to the Town Hall in the village, where we had been able to store the most needful stock of the school library books. Lady Swinton's two sons were in the forces and her two little grandsons were at the Hall all the time. Lord Swinton often came back for short spells from his duties as Minister for Air. The park, with its woodlands and several lakes and walled gardens, was a delight in all seasons, first with the show of daffodils, then the rhododendrons, and in the autumn the vivid colouring of the trees. The School spent hours de-heading the rhododendrons, lifting potatoes, cutting down thistles in the pasture land, and gathering wood. At first there was an attempt to play lacrosse on Lord Swinton's airstrip ground and some hockey was also played, but soon the equipment was not procurable and, since there were no matches, enthusiasm waned. Netball greatly improved and became an important game, and there were a few good tennis courts for the summer. Exercise time each afternoon was given over to runs, walks and bicycling. Nearly everyone had a cycle and was able to enjoy the very fine countryside. On the occasional day's holidays in the summer term we used to cycle to Ilton reservoir up on the moors. Here in the little tarn surrounded by the heather and country flowers those who could swim had a lovely afternoon, followed by a hectic (and often for the escorts very anxious) spin down the three-mile hilly road to the Hall again.

Canon Byron Scott was the vicar of Masham and a frequent visitor to School. Each Sunday morning the girls walked to the village to attend the morning service at the fine old church, and the matrons were just as particular to see that everyone was tidy, coats buttoned, hats and gloves on, as they had always been in Harrogate. Once or twice we squeezed into the Town Hall to see a film hired for the evening to entertain the soldiers. The sanatorium was in the old vicarage near the church and patients had to be driven down the dark country lane to be nursed there. Dr Campbell Ward, the school medical officer, came from Harrogate twice a week for the clinics and other cases: he must have found the twenty-mile journey, there and back in the winter weather, very arduous and exhausting at his time of life.

The dogs had a marvellous life in the country with rabbits everywhere and constant adventures. Once Miss Jacob's two dogs were lost in the snow on the moors for several days: many of the girls helped to search for them and this resulted in bad frost-bite on the legs for weeks afterwards, but the relief that the dogs were found was some compensation. The Canada geese on the Home lake were a frequent sight as they came in, high in the sky, to swoop down in a flock and alight on the water. The large herd of deer was soon very familiar and we became used to the baying and the rutting season and picking up antlers, and even sometimes finding a little fawn hiding in the long grass in early summer.

In the years 1942–44 every scheme which could be made to help the war

Main dining room, Swinton Hall. Gainsborough's Mme Bacelli and Romney's Lady Hamilton can be seen

effort was carried out with zest. The "Victory Service Clubs" became an important activity, particularly the camouflage netting when the army head-quarters had to be supplied with two or three nets a week. Sets of girls filled sandbags, and many did work on the farms; others collected firewood regularly for the old people in Masham. Household service, which included laying tables, cleaning carpets and form-rooms, was organised, and a great amount of knitting was accomplished. There was a salvage group and a National Savings group and a discussion group on such topics as explosives, medicinal herbs and poison gases. All these activities were recorded week by week to show the achievements of each section. The Guide company had an active life including much out-of-door work. Miss Bacon ran the company and also some Rangers. It was interesting to link the school company with that in Masham run by Miss Ebsworth, Lady Swinton's housekeeper and compa-nion. Even in the country it was felt necessary to have air-raid shelters in case of bombing, and part of the ha-ha near the Hall was covered and made secure with wooden benches lining the walls. On one or two alerts the School was marshalled into the shelters to spend very miserable, uncomfortable, cold hours underground. Later the shelters were not used and the girls descended to the lower floors and lay in serried ranks in their eiderdowns. There were practices with gas masks and every girl was sent through a tear gas chamber in an outhouse to test the efficiency of her mask.

None of us who were at Swinton could fail to realise what the School owed to Miss Jacob. Nothing was impossible to her (nor did she allow anything to be impossible for us or the girls). Throughout the six years we kept all the occasions and traditions of College ready for the time when we should return to Harrogate. Girls strove for and won many places at universities and training colleges: the lists are full of these successes, and some of the most accomplished of our Old Girls had all their education at Swinton. It is impossible to list these names, but in 1943 there were twelve girls at Oxford or Cambridge and thirty-six at other universities. It is perhaps of interest that the "garage" produced twenty-four of these, most of them going on to do medicine or other scientific work: one was Joan Barnes (Hastewell) who holds the position of treasurer of the Union.

The music flourished exceedingly, and there were concerts given by well known artistes, with music clubs, gramophone recitals and competitions within the School forming one of the main sources of entertainment. Miss Davies retired after the first year, and she, together with Miss Forde, went to live in a wing of Miss Jones' home in the Cotswolds. It must have been a strange retirement for them as they had been at the College since its beginnings and now had to see so much of what they had built up, confused and seemingly lost in a country mansion. Miss Williams took over the direction of the music and Miss Davies could not have had a more accomplished musician as her successor. The Christmas service was a feature at Swinton, with the tree in the hall, and the girls standing in tiers on the main stairs and balconies to sing *The First Nowell* and many old and new carols. The Passion Music was sung each year in Masham church to the large congregation of school and local residents. Later Miss Battye joined the staff for the piano and Miss Rowland for the violin, each contributing their own particular talents to the music.

The dramatic work under Miss Moss was very buoyant, giving many plays for the public and the parents which all had to be out-of-doors. A corner of the garden with a large rockery formed the setting, and the audience, wrapped in rugs and seated on the sloping ground, enjoyed it all as a respite from the war reports or the worries of home life. Miss Ruth Shaw was School secretary all the war years. A minute office was contrived for her with no room for files and very little daylight. Here she managed to keep the business of the school in excellent order, including all the end of term accounts. Mr Stone, the bursar, was called into the reserve navy. Miss Shaw and Miss Nora Hewlett, who came out from Harrogate each week to assist her, lived in a house in Park Street in the village. The HCU business was run by Dorothy Sibly for a while and later taken over by Mary Auty (Kingswell). There were no formal Reunions, but interesting details in the long lists of personalia show that there was no shortage of news of the Union members, most of whom were doing active war work.

Wartime cookery class in Swinton Harness room

Watching open air play at Swinton Hall

Tribute must be paid to Miss Shaw for all she did for the school and the Union. After helping to re-establish the College at Harrogate, she returned to her home in the Isle of Man after twenty-two years as secretary. She then for twelve years took over the organisation of the Union which, with her knowledge of members of all ages, was invaluable. For some years after that she still kept in contact with the overseas branch of the Union.

During all the time at Swinton Miss Jones kept in close touch with the School and as governor was able to give much help on the many problems. Lord Davidson also paid frequent visits, and Mr Adams, the secretary of the Allied Schools, was required to give constant advice on the business matters concerning the estate, our tenure and the links with Lord and Lady Swinton. Presumably detailed financial arrangements were made with the family both during and after the war, and the school had compensation from the Government for the use of the Harrogate buildings which were occupied by the Ministry of Aircraft production for five years. Oakdale was not commandeered. In the first year of the war all the lower fourth girls had to remain there as Swinton Hall could not accommodate the whole School. A house was bought in Kent Road and later another near Oakdale gate for overflows, and for a sick house. Miss Jacob visited Harrogate once a week as petrol was granted for essential journeys, while Miss Clarke, helped by Miss Thomas, Miss Millar, Miss Hull and matron Millen ran the junior department which had become for those years quite a big school.

THE POST-WAR YEARS AT HARROGATE

The War ended in 1945 and the College, which had been occupied by the Ministry of Aircraft production, was handed back that year. Dick Hammonds, the engineer and boilerman had remained in Harrogate, as also had Harold Newton the storeman and electrician. These "kept an eye" on the premises and were very valuable to the Ministry. Most of the College building was used by hundreds of designers and clerks who were employed on aircraft designs. The basement of Lincoln was given over to the photography and processing of blue prints of aeroplanes. Most of the workers were billetted in Harrogate and did not live in the College, but the kitchens were in use to provide daytime meals. The swimming bath had been used by Oakdale for the first year, but later was taken over to give instruction in rescue work for the Army. The passages under the bath had been used by us for storage of hundreds of pictures and other items which could not be taken to Swinton, but sadly during the last year or two all these precious things disappeared. The Ministry kept the external fabric of the school in good order but the inside became neglected and dirty and the electric wiring and heating installations were over-worked. When we returned, such matters were put right by squads of electricians and decorators, partly, but by no means entirely, paid for by Government compensation: the standard colour of paint issued was dull brown throughout! At the end of the war a year had to elapse before the College could return to its premises, and during that time all our efforts and thoughts were given over to planning this mammoth task.

Miss Jacob wrote in 1945 "When we leave Swinton next July we shall have completed seven years in our war-time home. Most members of the School will leave large slices of their hearts behind them—on Roomer Common, at Ilton, Fearby, Colsterdale, and in many other places in the lovely country round Masham, but above all at Swinton itself, with its wealth of trees and flowers, its bird life, its deer, its lakes gleaming in the sun or shrouded in the mist and frost of winter. In our plainer but much loved Harrogate setting we shall often think of our Swinton period and recall the kindness of our host and hostess during the war years." Lord and Lady Swinton tragically lost their elder son during the war and their second son some years later. Their grandsons David, who became the heir, and Nicholas Cunliffe-Lister, were babies during our stay, and were often seen about with their nurse. Lady Swinton took a great interest in the life of the school and came to the concerts and cricket matches and frequently gave away the prizes. She became a school governor when we returned to Harrogate and always remained a firm friend and counsellor. Amid the rejoicing that we were now to go back to College there was indeed a real sadness that we were to leave the park and the village and the kind friends at Masham. We had a farewell party for everyone at the end of the last summer term with music and dancing and speeches on the front lawn.

During the summer holidays the long trek began to get our property back to Harrogate. As I was very familiar with the College premises I, helped by Miss Bacon, was on duty in Clarence Drive for about six weeks to receive the daily two or three furniture vans which were loaded up at Swinton. Miss Jacob, Miss Brown and others arranged the loads, and every morning a telephone message would come through to me "I am sending you fifty beds, sixty chests of drawers and a set of pianos"! Slowly, day by day, College and the houses were refurnished. The men needed direction and encouragement, for it was hard work handling desks and wardrobes to the top floors and pianos to the music corridor. Loud were the wails later, when housemistresses found that some remembered "piece" had gone to Balliol instead of Armaclare or that Clarence had all the large white chests instead of little brown ones. Flooring was non-existent and unprocurable, and the "Back to College" House funds, which had built up from subscriptions from leavers for six years, were very welcome later to buy carpets for the common rooms or other things which had been lost or worn out. But the huge job was eventually completed in time for term to start in September, and for all my remaining time at College I was usually able to visualise every room and knew the whereabouts of all the different items of furniture.

Various alterations were made in the premises before we returned. The small single bedrooms on the first floor in the front of College were turned into one big room for the staff room, and a little more space was given to chemistry, physics, cookery and crafts. The two semi-detached houses at the corner of Clarence Drive were bought, one for the headmistress and the other for a staff house. A big house in York Road was vacated by the Women's Army and was bought as an extra boarding house and named Swinton, with the very large Godolphin garden between York Road and Clarence Drive also purchased as a retreat for any girls on summer evenings. Girls from different layers were asked to volunteer to found this new House, and Miss Willson, who had joined the PE department after her demobilization before we moved back, was its first housemistress, and under her excellent leadership it became one of the most successful Houses. A further change in the Houses was the use of former Clarence next to the playground, to provide extra bedrooms for Armaclare, since the Clarence girls had been absorbed into Lincoln under Miss Brown, while at Masham.

Of all the changes the most revolutionary was the introduction of central feeding, requiring a second large dining room for the outside Houses. Rationing was still enforced in the country and cooks could not be found to prepare meals in the boarding houses as had been the arrangement before the war. The only possible room for about two hundred girls was the assembly hall at the back, adjoining the kitchens, and this therefore became the North Dining Room from that date. The use of the room for meals left only the gymnasium (small hall) for everything else, assemblies, choral classes, gymnastics, dancing, concerts and drama. For about ten years the College had the greatest difficulty in organising its life for these occasions, as the room was very overcrowded and, moreover, there was a continual need for the girls to carry chairs to and from the dining rooms for all the different functions. One of the most urgent needs as soon as money could be raised and building permitted was to provide a new gymnasium or hall and thus relieve the congestion on that small room.

About one hundred new girls were admitted for September 1946 and none of the girls who were at Swinton had ever been in the Harrogate buildings. All the seniors arrived two days before the juniors and with the help of many direction notices prepared by Miss Sankey, they acquainted themselves with the whole of the school and were able to assist when the younger girls arrived. As can be imagined, the organisation of the chapel, house life, school life, meals, games and much else was intense, but we were fortunate that the housemistresses and many of the matrons had been with us before the war. Miss Lawson was head matron and amongst other things had much work to cover with regard to the uniform and the large second-hand department of clothes which had been collected when rationing began. On the return to College Jill Fraser was head prefect and the school was fortunate to have a girl of sterling moral calibre with an all-round interest in everything concerning the College, and also outstanding academic ability. Jill obtained an open scholarship to read science at Oxford and after five years there decided to join the staff of the pioneer African school at Achimota in Ghana. A few months after she started her work, so full of promise for her teaching and missionary service, she was killed in a car accident in a country road near that school. Her death was one of the great sorrows of Harrogate College.

During the war years at Swinton and later on return to Harrogate a number of members of staff gave the utmost of their time and inspiration to the School. Some of these are mentioned later in this book but I recall here some others. Miss Lainé was at the College in the early years of the 1920s and returned in the war to teach biology. She came back to Harrogate and was the much loved and valued housemistress of Lancaster until 1953. Miss Kay taught chemistry: she was an eminent teacher and one with a vast store of other knowledge and interests, all of which kept her pupils on their toes, resulting in many university successes. Miss Bickerdike taught mathematics and was housemistress of Armaclare: home circumstances in 1952 made it necessary for her to take another post at Nottingham High School but she never lost interest in the College and returned after retirement to "fill in gaps" both teaching and in Armaclare, and notably to install Swinton House in its new home in Clarence Drive in 1970. Miss Lowe (later Mrs Elliott), an English scholar, gave the school much enjoyment and amusement with her original writings, especially with the numerous topical plays she wrote for production while we were at Swinton. Jean Radford whose school life had been at College, came back in 1948 to run the art department, and both her pupils' work and her own personal art became a feature of the School. Many remember the wonderful Christmas decorations, the white Christmas tree in the chapel, the marvellous artistic decorations in the marquee when we had our huge bazaar and the scrolls which were given by her pupils to their friends or teachers on leaving. Miss Bertha Hodgson-Smith died at school in 1947. She had been history mistress for twenty-nine years and had stayed on to see the College back to Harrogate. Speaking of her in chapel Miss Jacob said:

"Her keen personal interest in the progress, moral as well as intellectual, of each girl, her vigilance for their individual needs and a readiness to grapple with the difficulties of many, have endeared her to successive generations of school girls". Much else was said of one whom we all, staff and girls, loved and respected, but this extract will serve to recall her memory to those who had the privilege of knowing her.

In 1950 a special memorial service was held in the chapel for the founder, George Mearns Savery on the centenary of his birth. Miss Jones gave a wonderful address. Fifteen former pupils of the boys' school 1885–1905 were present and a tribute was paid by the Rev H Mallinson who was secretary of the Old Boys' Union in 1895 and later a master of the School.

The life of the School from 1946–52 was almost entirely devoted to recovery from the war and the struggle to return to normal. We were crowded with girls, but the severe restrictions in all walks of life produced many obstacles. Rationing of food and clothes was still strict and even simple things such as crockery, school stationery, books, and wood for repairs could not be obtained. Hopefully we had thought to increase our accommodation with one or two outside classrooms, a new gymnasium and science and art departments, and to enlarge the chapel, but every attempt to do so was turned down by government orders. In the world, the aftermath of the war resulted, as was inevitable, in frustration, discontent and disillusion after the high hopes which victory had promised. The young people were bound to be affected by the general attitude, although in the sheltered atmosphere of a residential school the emphasis on work, music, games, competitions, and day-to-day interests kept the girls and staff happily busy: we were able to go to concerts and lectures in the Royal Hall in Harrogate, and the parents were again able to visit their children for some week-ends.

Unfortunately there was a big epidemic of scarlet fever in the first spring term after our return, and we had over a hundred cases in a few weeks. In those days this was a serious illness for young people, and there was no chance of nursing such numbers within the School. Girls were taken to the isolation hospitals at Harrogate, Knaresborough, Ripon and Menston in the "Black Maria" which called many times a week. Bedding and clothing had all to be "baked" at the disinfecting depot and books destroyed: Miss Lawson as head matron used to be seen fumigating yet another bedroom by burning a sulphur candle, before the cleaners could enter. We used to visit our girls at the various hospitals where we found them in large wards, very carefully and clinically nursed and under strict discipline! The sojourn in hospital was then for about five weeks. Dr Campbell-Ward who had been medical officer for twenty-three years retired in 1947 and handed over the work to his son Dr John Ward.

During the post-war years the speech day gatherings were held as before in a marquee on the field. At the first one Lord Swinton was the chief guest and part of his speech is worthy of record as he paid a tribute to the morale and discipline of the girls saying "You maintained an extraordinarily high standard of behaviour in our home; you never threw darts at my ancestors". In more serious vein he spoke of the grave problems of the world, the desire and need to bring freedom, and the urgent need for everyone to co-operate with each other, recognising duties as well as rights. "A planned economy is essential, but no system could relieve the individual of effort and responsibility. An ordered world in which men and women passively accepted work or position would not get us very far and it would be a dreary place into the bargain. Compulsory uniformity is more likely to produce the lowest common denominator than the highest common factor. Initiative is necessary for progress." Lord Swinton went on to speak of the great need for tolerance and the value of tradition "Unless a school has created a communion of fellowship and inspired a proper pride, then it is not much of a place, or more probably the pupils themselves have not played their part." Speech Days in the following years were addressed by Mr J T Christie, headmaster of Westminster School, Sir L Stone, Vice Chancellor of the Duchy of Lancaster, and Mr Holmes, the USA Minister in London, each with their own special message to the School.

The physical education progressed steadily and from beginning again in 1946 almost from scratch, the standard of lacrosse, cricket and tennis soon became notable again. The Duchy Club hard tennis courts were bought and gave six extra courts, and there were eight lacrosse pitches on the big field near Harlow. The swimming bath needed much repair but Miss Jones generously gifted the money and it was re-opened in 1947. The playground was badly cracked and damaged after its use as a fuel dump and lorry park, and was repaired to give some netball courts with a lower playground for lacrosse practice. At the speech day in 1948 Miss Jacob spoke with appreciation of the estate staff. "The gardens, under the care and design of the head gardener and his assistants, from the wilderness of three years ago, have been transformed into a neatness and pleasantness of varying colours which give delight to visitors and school alike, and the work of the groundsmen on our land is equally appreciated. The task of manning the twenty-three boilers with coke, each several times a day, is the responsibility of the three boiler men, who still have to work hard all summer to deal with the heating and maintenance of the swimming bath."

It is perhaps fitting to mention in this connection how fortunate the School has been in the continuity of service of the estate men.

Fred Newton in the early days looked after the horse which carried stores from house to house with the flat cart, and also pulled the mower over the field. The horse had to don its soft shoes for walking over the cricket pitch (the field at the back of College is still called "The Pitch" by many Old Girls of former times). Harold Newton, when he left school, came to help his father with stores and cartage and was trained as an electrician by the Ministry during the war years. His presentation tankard and watch report that he was with the College from 1931 to 1977. Percy Wright worked with his father, the joiner, in the joiner's shop at the back of Lincoln until he took over all the work in that department. Percy was at the beck and call of the staff for the innumerable repairs and contrivances everyone hoped he could accomplish, until he too retired in 1977. Dick Hammonds was in charge of the boilers and an expert on the plumbing in the College. His son Ken followed him, retiring now in 1980, leaving only Ray, the younger brother, to carry on the family supervision of the boilers, assisted by Joe Clarke who, with his wife Alice, have been with us since Swinton days.

Throughout the war years and afterwards, Oakdale preparatory section was very full and flourishing. Miss Clarke retired in 1947 and Miss Millen (Tron) in 1949. Tron had an amazing memory for names and characters and kept up contacts with many of her children to the end of her long life of ninety-four years. There were a few changes of personnel for a year or two until Miss Killingley and Miss Dare took over the charge of Oakdale in 1950.

In 1950 the governors invited a member of the Union to serve on the school council, and Dame May Curwen became the first of these governors. Since that time eight more of the Union have held this position, to the pleasure and appreciation of the chairmen. These representatives are voted into office by the HCU and up to now the following have had this honour: Sybil Toler (Murray), Isabel Herdman (Crawford), Mary Auty (Kingswell), Marjorie Morgan (Bartram), Rona McColl (Brown), Joyce Carter (Aikman), Nora Glenny (Grieve), Josephine Kingswell (Bankes). In 1948 the Union suggested that Miss Jacob should have her portrait painted to mark both her fifteen years as headmistress, and the School's jubilee. This was carried out by Mr Edward Halliday, later one of the Queen's portrait painters. The very fine likeness hangs in the School library.

In 1950 there was anxiety about Miss Jacob's health as she had some black-outs at times of pressure or overwork. These naturally disturbed the School and in the Autumn term of 1951 the governors asked Dame Emmeline Tanner, who had retired from Roedean some years previously, to act as headmistress while Miss Jacob was on sick leave. Dame Emmeline enjoyed returning to work and comparing Harrogate College with Roedean (often with many anecdotes): we all became fond of her, although as can be imagined it was not always easy to pursue with the regular routine as we thought necessary. Dame Emmeline did not find the Yorkshire climate, nor our somewhat spartan central heating, suited her, and unfortunately she became ill at Christmas time and had to spend some weeks in hospital, eventually returning to her more sheltered life and retirement. Meanwhile it came as a very great shock to the staff and girls when they learnt that the governors, acting on medical advice, felt it advisable for Miss Jacob to resign from her post as headmistress. She had been at College for seventeen years, covering both the war and post-war periods. They were days fraught with abnormal problems and anxieties, and Miss Jacob's leadership during that time had gained her the admiration and affection of everyone. For herself the next year or two were very sad, but we were very glad that she fully recovered, and was able to become head-mistress of Falmouth High School until her retirement.

In the spring and summer terms of 1952 I and my housemistress colleagues looked after the School while we waited the arrival of Miss Todd who was then headmistress of Durham High School and could not join us until September. The years 1951 and 1952 were I suppose some of the most worrying and difficult for the College, and it was with great pleasure that we welcomed Miss Todd, and the next phase in the history then began.

CHAPTER IV

Miss Todd's Headship

1952–1960

EXPANSION AND THE ENDOWMENT FUND

In appointing Miss Todd as successor to Miss Jacob the governors had changed their allegiance from Cambridge to Oxford and from classics to mathematics. The fact that Miss Todd also held a diploma in theology meant that she could the more easily carry on the chapel tradition that had been so firmly set by Miss Jones and continued under Miss Jacob. The new headmistress very soon established a happy relationship with both staff and girls and this was to continue throughout her twenty-one years at the College. They were to be years not only of progress and development in the school, but also of great educational change throughout the country.

1953 was a time of nationwide rejoicing during which the whole country celebrated the Queen's Coronation. Princess Elizabeth, called to high office at such an early age, captured everyone's imagination, particularly perhaps that of the younger generation who could only remember the austerities left from the war years as the world tried to adjust itself to changed conditions. The new reign was heralded as the beginning of a second Elizabethan Age, and for a while at least, hearts were high. It was an especially exciting year for Harrogate College, since, in addition to joining in the general rejoicing, it had its own Diamond Jubilee to celebrate. Ten years previously the Golden Jubilee had not gone by unnoticed, but in the middle of the most difficult war period it had of necessity passed without any appropriate commemoration being possible. Now, with the school back in its own building, the time of resettling over, and a new headmistress installed, there was nothing to prevent a lively spirit of optimism pervading the school, and this was present in all the celebratory functions that took place during that year. The first of these was the July speech day. The chairman, Lord Davidson, who was also Chancellor of the Duchy of Lancaster, suggested that as the College occupied Duchy lands it would be appropriate for us, on our sixtieth anniversary, to send loyal greetings to the Queen as Duke of Lancaster in this her coronation year. This was done, and, with the timing so characteristic of the Royal Family, an acknowledgement was received from Her Majesty in time for it to be read to the visitors before they departed. Also in the summer term, the school in patriotic vein sang and performed scenes based on German's *Merrie England*: the staff too distinguished themselves in a performance of *The Importance of Being 'Earnest'*, with Miss Brock an incomparable Lady Bracknell.

But the highlight of the year came in the autumn term when we were honoured by a visit from the Princess Royal. The occasion was the presenta- tion of the new entrance gates which were the jubilee gift of the HCU. The gates, in wrought iron, were the work of the Scottish Country Industries Development Trust and were designed by Charles Guthrie. It was a design in which dignified vertical bars carried the College crest in the centre, sur- rounded by a clover leaf motif. The effect was very pleasing and made a great difference to "first impressions" in approaching the school: the choice of gift could not have been happier and it met with universal appreciation. Her Royal Highness had graciously consented to come and declare the gates open during the HCU week-end, and a distinguished gathering was there to welcome her. She was accompanied by her lady-in-waiting Lady Paynter: the Bishop of Ripon was there to make the dedication and Lord Davidson, Mr Kenneth Adams and Miss Jacob were among the visitors. Sybil Murray, the HCU governor, formally presented the gates to the headmistress and she then handed the key to the Princess who turned it in the lock and walked through, declaring the gates to be open. She was given a bouquet of red roses by the head girl, Mary King (Miller) and then walked down the drive to the library where she was to have tea and where the VIPs and prefects were presented to her. It was a wonderful day, never to be forgotten by those who were able to be there, and the *Chronicle* of the time has some good photographs of the event. The key used by the Princess now hangs in the front hall of College. Later in the same day a historic HCU dinner was held at the Cairn Hotel— historic in the fact that the three headmistresses, Miss Jones, Miss Jacob, and Miss Todd, were all able to be present. There were many toasts and speeches and reminiscences went on far into the night.

In comparison with 1953 the following year was a quiet one. In the competi- tive world outside Diane Leather brought honours to the school by becoming the first woman to run an under-five-minute mile, clocking 4 minutes 59.6 seconds. Within our own more limited sphere we had a general inspection. The last such event had been in 1935. Since then a major war, necessitating evacuation and upheaval and a subsequent return and re-establishment had taken place, and the thought uppermost in the minds of those who remem- bered the days of crises was one of thankfulness, that after such vicissitudes the College should not only be still in existence to be inspected at all, but that it should be as flourishing and energetic as ever. It was a good time to have an inspection since, with post-war restrictions at last eased, it was time for

1953 The 60th Anniversary—the three Headmistresses greeting guests in the Cairn Hotel

The 60th Anniversary, opening of the gates

75

The 60th Anniversary, the Princess Royal takes tea with L Graham, M King,
J Kingswell, J Sawkill, A Turnbull, U Dodd

renovation and expansion. The representatives who came were not all familiar with the workings of a boarding school and the weekly time-table caused some amusement. The need to provide time for organised games and outdoor exercise in the daylight afternoons in the winter terms (no cycling or walking to school for boarders) and the need too to give a chance for relaxation and a cosy half hour round the common-room fire before the evening lesson period, had to be explained. A time had to be sacrosant for three hundred girls to wash their hair when the hot water system was arranged for this occasion, and there were indeed many other small details where home life as well as school life had to be fitted into the seven-day week. The Inspectors were very helpful with suggestions for desirable improvements in curriculum and buildings.

One of the first problems to be tackled, which had become even more urgent, was the chapel accommodation which had somehow to be increased to give room for the extra numbers. At this time College finances were, like those of other public schools, adequate for the efficient running of the school and the maintaining of existing fabric, but not for covering ambitious development schemes, and this meant that any extra project usually had to be preceded by a fund-raising effort. In the case of the proposed chapel extension a fund already existed, started a while previously by the HCU, and a campaign was now launched to augment it. It was decided that the only feasible solution was to move out the south wall, inserting an additional row of supporting pillars and creating an extra south aisle. The existing wall was first taken down, stone by stone and laid in place on the playground, so that for some weeks we viewed it in a horizontal position. The builders worked behind a tarpaulin, suspending operations for a few minutes each morning so that we could hold morning Chapel. As the work progressed we saw the pillars being brought in, the wall and windows re-erected and finally the new roof being put in place. Some of the work was done by stone masons from Ripon Cathedral as experts in such type of work. We waited with interest to see how the new aisle would blend with the rest of the chapel and when the tarpaulin was finally removed everyone was pleased with how perfectly it harmonised. The whole chapel was redecorated and new oak pews were added. Later there was to be a gift of three staff pews, given by the HCU in memory of Miss Gask, and these beautifully completed the furnishing of the west end. The successful execution of this difficult piece of work was due in no small measure to our architect Mr Creak and builder Mr Pilkington.

About this time a more mundane but very necessary extension took place in the kitchen regions. Since the return after the war the kitchen staff had struggled to feed the whole school from kitchens designed only for the York and Lancaster girls, and an extension was long overdue. The space available for development was very restricted, but it was possible to make some addition to the area and thus also to modernise the equipment.

The next development was influenced by what was taking place in the country at large. One of the effects of the Butler Act of 1944 had been an improvement in the standard of the primary schools, and it was accepted in principle that the natural change from primary to secondary education should come at eleven. Many parents, influenced also by economic considerations, began to keep their daughters at home until eleven, seeking entrance to their public schools at that age. Although Oakdale could admit a limited number into the top form, provision had to be made for others in the senior school, and it was decided to start a junior House at College for these children. Clarence, which recently had been used as "overflow" premises, seemed ideal for this purpose both for its size and for its central location: it was fortunate that a small dwelling in York Road behind Balliol came on the market at this time so that the "overflow" could be transferred there, and before long this house became solely an annexe of Lincoln and so took the name Lincoln Cottage. For five years, until further major changes involving the juniors had to be made, the new junior Clarence formed a happy and contented little group, doing very well. New class rooms were also built behind the main school to accommodate the extra numbers for lessons.

Some changes in the senior Houses took place during this time at College. In 1953 Miss Langrish, who had joined the staff as head of the science department, succeeded Miss Láiné as housemistress of Lancaster. Two years later the time had come for Miss Bold to retire. She had been appointed in 1928 to teach geography and ten years later became housemistress of Balliol, a position she was to hold with distinction for seventeen years. She was succeeded by Miss Nixon, head of the history department, who left after a few years to become headmistress of Bedgebury Park and later of St James', Malvern. I myself at this time handed on the housemistress-ship of York to Miss Humphries. I had looked after the House since 1934 and now needed to give the time to the general organisation in the School.

In 1957 we were very saddened by the death of one of our young Old Girls, Anne Turnbull (Prestige). Anne had had a brilliant career at school, head of Balliol, outstanding in all games, and captain of the Yorkshire girls' cricket team. She had gone up to Cambridge to read science and was married to a fellow student during her second year in early January: three days later she was killed in a climbing accident when on honeymoon in Scotland.

A happier event occurred later in the year when the Queen and the Duke of Edinburgh, on a visit to the Yorkshire Show, made a détour to include Clarence Drive on the Duchy Estate (the Queen's land) and stopped outside the gates which her aunt had opened some years earlier, to accept a bouquet of red roses from the school, presented by the head girl Fenella Hamilton-Turner (Billington). The carriage lingered sufficiently long for everyone to have a good view of the royal personages, and an excellent photograph, autographed by Elizabeth and Philip, hangs in a prominent place outside the headmistress's door commemorating the occasion.

1957 The Queen and the Duke of Edinburgh outside the School with
F Hamilton-Turner

No-one present at the 1957 Speech Day will ever forget the circumstances of that July afternoon when a cloudburst in the midst of the proceedings kept the visitors prisoners in the marquee for about three hours. The guest speaker was Mr Arthur Holt, MP for Bolton, husband of Kathleen Openshaw and father of Diana. The quotation that follows is an extract from the *Chronicle*: "Mr Holt then presented the prizes, and during this time the skies grew blacker and the outlook more ominous. The storm broke simultaneously with the introductory sentences of his address, and with such fury that proceedings had to be suspended until the noise lessened. The marquee, which held over 1 300, stood up magnificently to the elements, but no canvas structure could have remained quite impervious to such an onslaught, and lines of gaily coloured umbrellas began to appear where the different sections of the roofing joined. The platform party was in a fortunate position and were able to appreciate in full the spectacle before them. As the rain lessened, Mr Holt essayed to begin. It was obvious, he said, that neither he nor his audience would be able to escape for some time, and on him he felt now lay the burden of the entertainment. He hoped that he would be relieved by the school at half-time, perhaps during the evening. He then gave a magnificent illustration of a Member of Parliament's skill in talking out time, doing it so well that everyone wanted more! In time everyone was able to escape from the marquee. The rain had subsided to a drizzle by early evening, and the girls, nothing daunted, were determined to attempt their much rehearsed Mass Drill, giving what was described as a "spirited performance". Every green cotton tunic soon bore a dark brown patch behind, distinguishing the effect from that of any other display before or later. The last word on what was to be a long remembered day came from one of the juniors: "How lucky we were able to do the Mass Drill after all. We didn't mind the puddles, of course, but we didn't much like the worms".

The next year, 1958, saw the launching of the Endowment Fund. Much building needed to be done and the project was an ambitious one with a new all-purpose assembly room cum gymnasium as first priority. The actual launching ceremony for the appeal took place in July with the vice-chancellor of Leeds University, Sir Charles Morris, as the principal speaker, and the HCU reunion was held the same week-end. It was decided that the Endowment Fund would remain permanently open "for the furthering of desirable projects as they arose". As a result of efforts made prior to the appeal the fund was able to start with a nucleus of £15 000 either in cash or in covenants, and the first objective was to augment this to £50 000.

The following year was to prove a busy and eventful one. With the prospect of a new hall it was now possible to tackle the problem of dining accommodation, making the North Dining Room (assembly hall) more suitable for its altered purpose. The room was increased in size by means of an extension built out northwards towards the field, and the floor level was raised to assist with the movement of trolleys in relation to the kitchen hatches. Few people will realize that a beautiful wooden dance floor still exists three feet below the surface of the present floor.

A fête to crown all fêtes was held in the summer in aid of the Endowment

Fund. It was the result of a full year's hard work in which members of the school, past and present, and many parents, participated. Our net spread far and wide and we had an astonishing collection of valuable things for sale, many gifted by fathers from their factories and spheres of work. An outstanding contribution came from Messrs Forsyths of Edinburgh, our outfitters, who presented a large doll, complete with trunk and every item of the familiar green and red uniform in miniature. In order to recapture some of the excitement and enthusiasm of the day it seems worth quoting from the *Chronicle* of that year. "We had fourteen stalls altogether and each of these was organised by three members of staff assisted by one girl from each house. Three days before the fête the vast marquée was erected on the cricket pitch, fixed into an iron-like substance after the continual baking it had received during the hot summer. The stalls were put in position and beautifully decorated in a scheme designed by Miss Radford. The day after the erection it poured without ceasing. In the evening of that day a huge rent appeared in the 'big top' and we wondered if all our newly built stalls would be razed to the ground if the tent had to be exchanged for a new one. However a large patch repaired the damage, and the next day was fine." After a detailed description of stalls, sideshows, raffles and other arrangements, all made with the unashamed aim of extracting as much money as possible from the good-natured visitors, the account continues "It was interesting to stand on the fringe and watch the satisfied customers emerging from the tent with their purchases, and entertaining also to watch the fathers, whose function often seemed to be to sit on the grass guarding these purchases while the mothers went for more. A word must be said about the cashiers: three 'bankers' sat in a small tent from 1 pm to 6 pm faced with bushels of pennies and other coins (4 000 sixpences) and of course hundreds of notes. They saw nothing but money for all those hours and produced a detailed balance sheet the day after the fête, showing that it had realised £3 600. This included a contribution of £1 000 received that morning from Miss Jones, together with her message of good wishes. Wandering round the pitch at bedtime on that summer's evening, it did indeed seem remarkable that everyone, and everything, had disappeared: not even a scrap of paper or a carton was visible: only the worn grass, where many feet had trod, remained, and the fête was over."

The prize-giving of that summer was a particularly happy one when the guest speaker was an ex-headmaster, Mr A Dobson. An octogenarian, although none could have believed it, he entertained us delightfully with an excellent speech, both witty and wise.

In recalling that year, mention must be made of an outstanding production of "Everyman", presented in the chapel, which formed a perfect setting for such a play. To take on the interpretation of a morality play requires courage, but the rewards are correspondingly great. In this case Miss Robinson, the producer, was assisted by Miss Williams with the music, and Miss Sankey with the elaborate properties, and the result was a performance which made a lasting impression on those who saw it. Another event in the chapel took place in the summer holidays on a lovely sunny day, when a wedding was celebrated there for the first time, by special licence from the Archbishop. The occasion was the marriage of Ann Sugden (1947-55). Ann's two sisters Mary and Elizabeth were among the eight bridesmaids. Ann's grandmother, Ethel Roberts (Sugden) had been one of Miss Jones' original pupils, so the family connection with the College had been a long one.

GOODBYE TO MISS JONES

The greatest event of the year 1959 came in the Autumn Term, and it belonged primarily to Miss Jones and the HCU. 28 October, designated *Dies mirabilis* in the *Chronicle*, was Miss Jones' ninetieth birthday, and the Union felt that it must be suitably commemorated. It was decided to hold a celebratory luncheon in London to which all Old Girls who had been at College during Miss Jones' time should be invited. Ruth Shaw, who was the HCU general secretary, and two London members, Joyce Carter (Aikman) and Adza Hodgins (Vincent) undertook the arrangements, and the result was an unforgettable function enjoyed by everyone, not least by Miss Jones herself.

The following extracts written by Miss Davies describe how it was spent: "The big social event was a gala luncheon at the Hyde Park Hotel, London, attended by nearly three hundred members of the HCU, some former members of staff, and a few friends. Miss Jones and her sister Lady Bell (Lena) stayed at the hotel for the previous night, where masses of flowers, letters, telegrams, parcels and callers contributed to the excitement. Brian Johnston of the BBC came to record an interview which was to be heard on the early morning programme, and many Old Girls were surprised and delighted to be wakened unexpectedly by the well-known voice. Before the party Miss Jones received two special gifts from the Union. One was a brooch of the HCU badge in rose diamonds and rubies, accompanied by a beautiful card, the work of Jean Radford, and the other a special presentation copy of the biographical tribute (this had been compiled by Miss Davies) sponsored by pupils of her own period at Harrogate College. When the guests had taken their places for the luncheon the sonorous voice of the Master of Ceremonies rang out 'Ladies, upstanding please for the entrance of the Guest of Honour' and the familiar slight figure took her place. The formal proceedings were purposely kept short and the speeches limited to three. Miss Todd, as president of the HCU, welcomed the Guest of Honour warmly and felicitously, and conveyed the good wishes of the present school, and the toast to Miss Jones was proposed by Sybil Murray MBE, permanent member of the HCU on the governing body, who voiced the loving wishes and congratulations of all former pupils. After the toast had been honoured, Miss Jones rose to speak amid tumultuous applause."

Miss Jones began by reading out the letter of congratulation she had received that morning from the Minister of Education. She spoke for half an hour, at time reminiscing, at times philosophising, at times looking forward as it were with the school she had created, into the unknown future. The old spell was on her audience again as it had been so often in the past.

"My many birthdays with you have left me with wonderful memories—the

1959 Miss Jones' 90th birthday party in the Hyde Park Hotel. From right to left, Dame M Curwen, Mrs Murray, Mrs Crawford, Miss Sibly, Miss Todd and at the end Mrs Kingswell, Miss Shaw.

Miss Jones on her 90th birthday with sister Lena, J Kingswell and A Hodgins

gaiety, the youth and beauty of my dear girls and the sheer happiness that pulsated in the air. Is it strange that at times I feel lonely when I look back on the days when I was surrounded by you all, a gay, lively and youthful crowd? I remember two birthdays particularly because they were connected with the chapel building fund. On the first, the head girl, Margaret Luis, who is here today, handed me a cheque with the best wishes of the School, to open the fund: I looked at it and gasped; it was for £500. On the second, some years later, another cheque was given to me to close the fund and leave the chapel free from debt. What a boon the chapel has been to all the school—above all price. In looking back I find myself thinking in decades, 1904-1914, 1914-1924, 1924-1934. How quickly those years have passed; "gone like a puff, happy and over and short enough."

Finally came the thanks of the assembly to Miss Jones for her presence and her inspiring address. These thanks were expressed by Mary Kingswell who had recently begun her term of office as the HCU governor in succession to Isabel Crawford. The proceedings then ended, the Master of Ceremonies called for upstanding, and Miss Jones walked smilingly past her old girls to the wonder and admiration of all. But she had still another task to perform before she left for home, for she had been asked by the BBC to supplement her sound broadcast by a television appearance in the "Tonight" programme. This pre-recorded picture and interview by Mr Cliff Michelmore were done at the TV studios before she left London, and immediately afterwards she returned to Eastbourne in a BBC car, arriving home tired but happy.

Back in the quiet of her home Miss Jones was able to relive at her leisure every moment of her great day and to re-read her many letters and messages. That she had been able to enjoy everything to the full was obvious from letters which she herself wrote during the next month. In particular one to her nephew Mr Beaudeau Taggart in Ireland, written on 1 November, bubbles over with excitement as she graphically and humorously describes what had taken place. "The grand old toastmaster who would address me as 'my lady' in public and 'dearie' in private," had evidently taken her fancy. She really was, she said, a happy and fortunate nonogenarian. How she would have enjoyed poring over the *Chronicle* record of all that had happened to her that day.

Alas, that was not to be. As November moved into December it became obvious that Miss Jones was not well, and on 10 December, the day the *Chronicle* was due to go to press, news came that she had died. Thus that 1959 *Chronicle* took on a different significance to its readers. Miss Jones always loved quotations and was fond of using them. Perhaps she would have liked the one used by Miss Todd in her final tribute: "Busy with many lives: weaving them into multiform patterns with strands of diverse colours: evolving the hidden gift: freeing the imprisoned power: led, step by step by the wisdom of the Spirit".

A memorial service was held in chapel the following May in the presence of a large and representative gathering which included Miss Jones' sister Lena and her two brothers. Lord Davidson, chairman of the governors, read the extract "Valiant-for-Truth crosses the river", from *The Pilgrim's Progress*, as one of the Lessons.

CHAPTER V

Miss Todd's Headship

1960–1973

DEVELOPMENTS AND CHANGES

The School entered the next decade quietly confident in the ability to survive the problems that were confronting the public schools at that time, involved in its own new developments that were taking place as the building programme took shape. But in the world as a whole the sixties were to prove troubled years, and not an easy time in which to grow up. In retrospect it was to become known as the permissive age—a time when traditional standards began to be questioned, when rock-and-roll at its most boisterous set the style in the dance hall, when the world was invaded by the mini-skirt, when it was fashionable to be long-haired, unkempt and scruffy, and when to be tidy was considered "square". In the face of the violent social change that became the order of the day everything was queried. "Student power" began to manifest itself, and the insidious "generation gap" phrase was heard more and more frequently in television and in the press. Small wonder that parents at times felt bewildered and uncertain as to what line to take, and that many young folk were similarly out of their depth in a situation where moral absolutes were discounted and where the media, now such an inescapable influence, encouraged everyone to "express themselves" in any way that took their fancy. Meantime a great deal was happening in the general educational world. Challenging new ideas were being put forward, and as often happens in a period of change, the pendulum in some cases swung too far; but it was an exciting time in which to be in the classroom, and when enthusiasm and idealism were tempered with experience, the outcome was good. The increasing use of visual aids and tapes revolutionised teaching: the introduction of modern maths convulsed the mathematics department: "Nuffield Projects" invaded the sciences, and laboratories became popular in the teaching of languages. With all these new developments and innovations the time-honoured discipline of thorough learning fought for survival. As it moved with the times, Harrogate College remained faithful to the three Rs as necessary basics. The learning of tables was still imposed; the house spelling cup with its weekly dose of twenty new words was fiercely contested each term, and the value of a good literary style was not forgotten. All this paid dividends, needless to say, in later years, and original contributions to the Clover leaflet frequently showed undoubted merit.

In the sixth form the curriculum was broadened to include a wider range of general studies relevant to the problems of the time, and additional subjects such as Russian, economics and civics were added to the options available. The dramatic growth in the number of universities and polytechnics that took place in the sixties made entrance there easier and more popular, and most upper sixth girls went on after A-levels, to years of further education. The variety of careers becoming available to girls was also becoming wider.

All public schools were affected by the changing external climate. In the wider context it was a time when the whole ethos of the independent school was being challenged. A critical, even hostile, Government talked first of "abolishing" the public schools and later of "integrating them into the system". To this end the "Public Schools Commission" was set up, its purpose being to collect information to support this thesis. Groups of educationalists visited selected schools, and questionnaires were sent to others. Harrogate College was one of the first girls' schools to be visited, and the three delegates who came were given freedom to wander at will. After three days of "fact finding" and much interesting and provocative discussion, all were agreed on the one fact that there was no simple solution. The report, when it did appear, was subsequently "shelved", and with it, for the time being at least, the threat that had troubled those concerned with independent education.

There were various factors that influenced Harrogate College as it moved through the sixties. The widespread use of the motor car in preference to the trains made homes more accessible, and the sundry leaves of absence, pre-viously spent in the precincts of the school, gave way to a half-term break sufficiently long to allow everyone to spend the time away, thus keeping them in closer contact with their home environment. The introduction which had recently taken place of day pupils, tended also to loosen what had been a tight-ly knit community. The "boy friend" was of course a universal phenomenon, and debates and dances were held with neighbouring schools. Driving lessons were available for sixth forms: many visits were made to outside functions, and in this the College could take advantage of the facilities offered by Harrogate. Team games fell out of favour with many of the seniors: cricket was replaced by athletics. As more "freedom" became the order of the day, permission to wear home clothes when not in lessons, at first the prerogative of the sixth form, was gradually extended to the younger girls. In this respect the mini-skirt vogue caused one or two problems, as did the maxi which briefly followed it. One picturesque occasion comes to mind when the lacrosse

1962 opening of the Memorial Room with Miss Todd, Mrs Murray, Mrs Crawford, Miss Shaw

team set out to conquer London, with its extra sturdy "goalie" in the briefest of minis, the centre-attack wearing a velvet maxi, and a third member, who had concentrated on millinery, sporting a floral creation worthy of Ascot. But these episodes served to lighten the atmosphere, and there were times when the girls even laughed at themselves. Through it all it was interesting to notice the sanity with which the school as a whole reacted to the pressures of this era, and seemed to realise that freedom could only operate in a framework of order. Albeit there were signs also of a deeper unrest: the sense that in a troubled world it was an uncertain future that lay ahead, when, in a nuclear age, even survival was at stake. Social problems of which previous generations of youngsters had had little knowledge, challenged them, and these were debated with intensity and sincerity. Most girls worked hard, and everyone planned a career. Work involving "people" was much preferred. Many girls were interested in social work and a number were involved in projects of social welfare in Harrogate.

With the Endowment Fund steadily increasing, the first pegs to mark the position of the new assembly hall appeared during 1960, and the building was ready for use before the end of 1961. The main room was equipped as a modern gymnasium with movable stage for concerts and other occasions, and it was originally intended that what is now known as the Memorial Room should be a cloakroom and changing room: it may not be known that buried under the floor there still lie the drainage pipes for that scheme. However, the HCU, seeking a suitable memorial for Miss Jones, asked if they could be allowed to take over the room and be responsible for its decoration and complete furnishing in her memory, so plans were changed and their suggestion

Opening of the New Buildings with Miss Todd, Lady Swinton, Mr Creak (architect),
Lord Davidson

was accepted. Gordon Findlay was commissioned as adviser, and the attractive room as it exists today was the result. At the same time Mr C A Jones, brother of Miss Jones, and a former College bursar, generously provided the money to cover the cost of the complete colonnade which was to link the hall with the outer classrooms and the main school. The new buildings were officially opened by the Countess of Swinton on speech day 1962, with the prospect of the science block to follow in the succeeding year.

As has happened from time to time throughout the school's history, property in Clarence Drive was bought as soon as it came on the market, and the last pair of semi-detached houses, No 17 and 19 became available in 1962. This gave the College the continuous line from the Duchy Road corner down to Armaclare, with the large stretch of gardens behind, and with Swinton House more remote in York Road. With increasing numbers entering the school we were then able to start an eighth senior house, and Clarence once more changed character and became the House's new headquarters, with an overflow across the road in No 17. The eleven-year-old junior children who for five years had occupied Clarence were henceforth admitted direct to their senior Houses. The new Clarence was founded by volunteers, adopting as its emblem the phoenix, rising from the ashes, and thanks to the efforts and enthusiasm of Mrs Boddy who was in charge, and of Gillian Brown (Underhill), the first head of House, it thrived from the start and soon became a stable and successful entity.

Miss Jones had built up the school from small beginnings, but for her the most important and beloved acquisition had always been the chapel. Two years after her death her friends Miss Davies and Miss Forde approached the governors and asked for permission to replace the windows in the east end of the chapel with stained glass, as their personal memorial to her. They recalled that it had always been her wish that one day when funds permitted stained glass should be introduced. By this time, however, some people had grown to like the chapel as it was, and when the suggestion was made there were two very definite points of view. To solve the problem Dr Milner White, Dean of York, and one of the leading authorities on stained glass, was consulted. His verdict, as he gazed round the chapel, was that young people and colour go together; that it was good to have something inspiring to contemplate as an alternative when the sermon was dull, and moreover that the proposed windows would actually beautify the chapel. The gift was therefore accepted, and the London firm of Goddard and Gibbs was commissioned to do the work, with their senior architect and designer, Mr A E Buss in charge. We were able to visit the London workshop and were initiated into the fascinating world of stained glass. The theme of the window was chosen by Miss Davies and Miss Forde. The central of the three lights depicts Jesus as the Light of the World and the ones on either side show incidents in the life of St Andrew and St Paul, the first disciple and the first missionary. A beautiful small nativity scene was introduced at the bottom of the centre lancet, and the subsidiary decorations, chosen with infinite care by Miss Davies, all have symbolic meanings. It is a work of great delicacy and at once became the focal

The Memorial East Windows in the Chapel

point of the chapel. The changing colour effects, varying from hour to hour as the sun's rays alter their slant, are a constant source of fascination and wonder. Dedicated at the same time as the window was a fine organ screen, given by a group of Miss Jones' former pupils, carved in oak to match the other woodwork in the chapel, the work of Messrs Thompson of Kilburn.

Two years later the stained glass west window above the gallery was presented to the College. The generous donor was Jenny Train (Lang) who on a visit to the school was impressed by the beauty of the new memorial window and offered to give the west one in appreciation of all the chapel had meant to her in her schooldays. Mr Buss, who while busy on the east window had sometimes looked wistfully at the opposite one, was summoned immediately to take on the new project. We chose the four Evangelists as an appropriate theme. Each of the lights embodies a full length picture of one of the four, with his symbol above his head, and a scene taken from his particular gospel beneath. The carved area above is filled with angels and sun and moon to represent the linking of the spiritual with the earthly. Below are engraved the words "Thy word is a lamp unto my feet and a light unto my path" and in the bottom right hand corner is the family crest of the donor. As before we were impressed with the sensitive artistry of Mr Buss's work and proud indeed to possess two such wonderful windows. Very sadly Jenny Lang died in 1970 and a plaque to her memory was placed in the chapel, but the west window will always be her abiding memorial.

The West Windows
in the Chapel

I had helped to draw provisional plans for a new science department about 1936 before the war. We had struggled to teach all chemistry and physics in the one small "science" room in the main school, and adapted a classroom in the new wing teaching block for biology. The garage had been used for six years at Swinton and it was indeed a very great excitement to me personally, and to the other scientists when we were given the go-ahead to start the block in 1963. The previous year we had been able to provide a much needed biology room on the Clarence Drive frontage between Clarence and Woodlands as the beginning of the scheme. Before the main block could be built the ground adjoining the lower playground had to be cleared by the demolition of the ancient but much used "Cottage" which had had many functions, latterly cookery and crafts, and it was only when the handsome large building began to take shape that everyone became reconciled to the disappearance of this familiar land mark. There was the problem that any building with frontage in Clarence Drive had to be built in stone matching that already there, and for a while 400 tons of stone brought from some old recently vacated Yorkshire dwellings, lay piled in the Lincoln playground. The building provided five laboratories and subsidiary preparation rooms, two crafts rooms with a kiln room, and a large kitchen for cookery teaching, at last giving the school the practical rooms that had been so badly needed for many years. A descriptive plaque designed by Jean Radford was inset into the main wall. With the completion of this project we felt at the time that the major objectives of the Endowment Fund appeal had been achieved, and that we could not in any case expect more help from the parents of the day who had already been so generous with their donations and covenants. It was very satisfactory that there was so much to show for all the efforts that had gone into the many bazaars, coffee mornings, shows and other events that had taken place. At this point we must again acknowledge our indebtedness to Mr Creak, our Allied Schools architect, and to our contractor, the late Mr Wrightson. The personal and almost fatherly interest that Mr Wrightson took in our enterprises over the years was of great encouragement and help, and it was moreover reflected in all his workmen, who shared his enthusiasm. At Christmas time 1964, after the school had gone home, we held a grand party in the dining room when everyone who had been employed sat down to a celebratory dinner and Mr Creak came from London for the occasion, and there were some very pleasant speeches and presentations.

The next few years, as always, were crowded with internal affairs: matches, competitions, music and drama events, filled every term. We began to invite parents to regular Saturday morning meetings when topics of school interest were discussed, and the visitors were given opportunity to express their views. The practice of holding speech day in a marquée on the field was given up in favour of the Royal Hall which provided more space and comfort for everyone. The commemoration service during the summer term had been held, first at St Mary's and later at St Peter's, but latterly at the large church of St Wilfrid's just opposite the College. Mr Barker, the vicar of South Stainley had become school chaplain after the war and he was later succeeded by Canon Towell who was also much appreciated as a teacher of classics, eventually leaving to become residentiary Canon of Bradford Cathedral. In 1968 Canon Manktelow took over the chaplaincy, relinquishing it, to the school's regret, after nine years, when he became Bishop of Basingstoke.

In 1963 the time came for Miss Willson to retire. During her seventeen years she had not only been responsible for the launching of Swinton House but had also played a large part in re-establishing the physical work after the war. Before long every branch of the department was flourishing and a particularly high standard was reached in lacrosse and swimming. Very few regretted the passing of cricket from the scene, although it roused memories among former pupils, but athletics were now considered to be a more congenial and profitable way of taking exercise and it was one in which many girls could excel. A number of seniors however openly disliked team games and for them a large variety of alternatives was possible. With the departure of Miss Willson, Mass Drill, so long an annual spectacle, disappeared, to be replaced by more contemporary forms of display.

Miss Williams retired from the music department in 1964. She had joined the staff in 1926 and succeeded Miss Davies as director of music, a position which she held with great distinction for twenty four years. Her work for the school is best summarised by what was written by her friend and colleague, Miss Rowland, herself an outstanding violinist. "In Miss Williams we had a musician of rare excellence, with a great gift for teaching. She lavished her skill and experience on all her pupils, many of whom became accomplished musicians, whilst in those of lesser ability her infinite patience and encouragement produced results which often surprised the performers themselves. Choral practices, sprinkled as they were with pithy observation and with little gems of philosophy, were enjoyable and exhilarating experiences. Miss Williams is probably most widely remembered for the beauty of the music of the chapel services and for her fine training of the choir, whose singing revealed a subtle spiritual quality." Many girls were inspired to continue their training in singing, and of these two come to mind: Elizabeth Simon was awarded one of the first Kathleen Ferrier Scholarships and became internationally famous, and Maureen Keetch (Carpenter-Turner) delights many audiences in concerts and opera. Miss Williams was on the staff for thirty-eight years and will always hold a special place in the annals of the school.

She was succeeded as director of music by Mr H L Pope, under whose guidance the choir maintained its reputation, including amongst its activities two highly successful concert tours in Holland: it also broadcast, was recorded and televised, and took part in a variety of public events, including the singing of evensong in York Minster and Ripon Cathedral on several occasions. Both sub-choir and junior choir flourished and an interest in orchestral work was stimulated by the introduction of class violin lessons to the juniors both at Oakdale and in the senior school.

One certainty in an organisation of the complexity of Harrogate College is that there will always be something requiring renewal, and in 1965 it was the turn of the chapel organ. Some years previously it had had an overhaul, but now began to show signs of wear and tear. By a happy chance the decision to replace it coincided with the appointment of Mr Pope: he was an FRCO and

The Chapel,
dismantling the
old organ

The Chapel,
the new organ
and the screen

well versed in organ matters. A chapel organ fund was opened to be known as COF and for the next year or two all fund-raising efforts were concentrated on "doing something for COF". The response was gratifying and we were able to realise our aim, which was to have the new organ installed in time for the seventy fifth anniversary celebrations. Messrs Walkers of London were asked to build the instrument. Those of us who watched the dismantling of the old organ felt sad as we witnessed its removal: it had cost £500 in 1924 and was now sold for £100. The fact that the new organ cost about £7 500 is an indication of the changing values of the currency. Our adviser was Dr Francis Jackson of York Minster, and he strongly advocated a classical, as distinct from the former romantic, organ. It was the first of its kind in the north and attracted a great deal of interest and publicity. The opening concert, given by Dr Jackson himself, was recorded by the BBC, and many visitors have come to hear and see the organ since then.

The next department that required attention was the library which for some time had been inadequate for the needs of the school. To deal with this the side windows of the old library were removed and an extension built out onto the playground. At the same time the adjoining "glass porch" entrance was altered and improved. All the tables, chairs, bookcases and other library furnishings of the new room were gifted by various members of the school. The librarian, Miss Morgan (now Mrs Kirby) was inspired at the same time to add to her housemistress and chapel duties the work of introducing the Dewey Decimal System of cataloguing, an ambitious piece of work which took some months to complete.

Two other additions in building were made in 1970 and were the last to be undertaken during the time covered by this history. After the death of Miss Davies, Miss Forde and Lady Bell, the HCU presented a chapel porch in their memory. This not only makes a fitting memorial to these benefactors but also from a practical point of view is a great improvement to the west entrance of the chapel.

The last project, which had the School's whole-hearted approval, was the erecting of the squash courts. A bazaar was held in the summer, funds increased encouragingly by efforts from all the Houses, and two very fine courts were soon in use. The game became popular, and it was not long before the standard of play had reached a very creditable level.

1968 was the school's seventy fifth anniversary. In May of that year between four and five hundred of the HCU with an age range of seventeen to eighty seven, gathered to spend a commemorative week-end together, the highlight being a luncheon in the Cairn Hotel. Miss Jacob had journeyed from Falmouth to be present, and two of the oldest members Marion Talbot (Auty) and Birdie Brailsford (Booth) were among those specially welcome: both belonged to Percy Lodge days and both were mothers and now grandmothers of old girls. Also amongst the distinguished company, several of whom were public figures, was Sybil Murray, well known in educational and other fields in Scotland, and now, after many years of association with Harrogate College in a variety of ways, chairman of our governing body. There were toasts and replies, all received with acclaim, Esmée Carter (Lunn), in an inspiring speech which was reported in full in the *Chronicle*, proposed the toast of the school. Reminding those present of the standards set by Miss Jones, and proudly maintained by her two successors, she contrasted those ideals with the "everyone for herself" philosophy of the permissive age. It was for us to guard our traditions and to see that our school, so greatly loved, should continue to survive and flourish for future generations. In her reply Miss Todd referred to messages she had received from former members, including an amusing one from one Old Boy, and she also gave news of present day events, thus linking past with present in happy sequence. I myself had the honour of proposing the toast of the HCU, to which Isabel Crawford replied. In lighter vein I am tempted to quote, as I did then, some lines that had been written by Miss Davies a long time ago, and which struck a note which appealed to the large concourse of Old Girls in nostalgic mood, brought together for a weekend of memories:

"I wish I'd been a better girl when I was at HC:
I wish I'd loved my teachers wise (do they wish they'd loved me?).

I wish I'd used my talents small till they became immense:
Instead of being quite content to be considered dense.

I wish instead of raucous shouts in form room or on field
I'd used my voice with vocal art and music's soul revealed.

I wish I'd kept the Rules and Regs constructed for my good:
The love for deeds of naughtiness unselfishly withstood.

I wish I'd brought my parents dear, reports for their elation,
In which the staff described my work with glowing admiration."

And the rhymes ended with a homily to the present girls

"Your teachers dear, always revere
And work with endless ardour
Thus you will rise, to your surprise
Till you can go no farther."

The preacher at the commemoration service held the following day was the Rt Rev A Hoskyns-Abrahall, Bishop of Lancaster, and husband of Margaret Storey. His address, strikingly appropriate for the occasion, gave the congregation plenty on which to ponder. The present school's turn for celebrations came on Speech Day when the Duke of Devonshire was the guest of honour. Sir Stanley Harley, chairman of the central committee, was present, accompanied by Lady Harley, and so also were Mr Bateman, who had succeeded Mr Adams as general manager, and other members of the central committee and most of our governing body. Many of the large number of visitors were seeing the new buildings for the first time and spent a busy day inspecting them and the various exhibitions arranged for their entertainment. The school gave a colourful display of Israeli and East European dancing on the field, and the evening was spent by watching a performance of the play by Alvarez Quintero, "The Women have their Way", a title considered appropriate for the occasion.

In a community such as ours there are sadly bound to be tragic losses, and it was a great shock to hear of the death in March 1969 of Nicola Millar, one of our most promising former pupils. Nicola was a Scholar of the School, head of her House and a member of the choir, and studied law at Bristol University. She had become a barrister and had just been awarded a Winston Churchill Pupillage Prize when she was killed in a car accident at the age of 23. The two flowering cherry trees in the College front lawn were given by her parents in her memory.

During the summer the Harrogate Festival of Arts asked if they might stage their flower festival in the school and this took place in August when for the space of a week the rooms were magically transformed by the introduction of a great variety of wonderful floral displays. It was interesting to find what a fine setting the College (even the main stairs) made for the whole enterprise, and there was a constant stream of visitors who seemed to enjoy the opportunity of seeing the inside of the school almost as much as viewing the actual displays.

An amusing event also occurred when Harrogate College was invited to supply 20–30 juniors to become the pupils of Lowood School in a TV production of *Jane Eyre*. We had difficulty in selecting suitable girls, as they had to look scared, skinny and undernourished! To capture the mood of the story they could only be filmed when the weather was dull and miserable, and on such days they were transported to their location in the wilds of North Yorkshire. Before setting off they came to chapel arrayed in the demure charity dresses and bonnets of the period, imparting a picturesque Victorian atmosphere to our morning prayers.

ENTERING THE SEVENTIES

As we approached the seventies it was becoming apparent that reorganisation was needed at both the junior and the very senior ends of the School. From time to time in the story there have been references to the preparatory department at Oakdale. In the very early days a group of younger children was housed in Woodlands as part of the senior school, and it was in 1916 that the Oakdale estate was acquired and the preparatory department became a separate entity. It was an unusually attractive house set in 20 acres of grounds, and it made an ideal home for 40 or so little girls. Miss Lena Jones took up residence there and remained in charge until 1935 when she retired at the same time as her sister. From all accounts they were idyllic years and few children could have had a happier introduction to school life. 'Miss Lena' loved and mothered her young charges and everything—or nearly everything—was 'fun'. She had a strong personality and a boundless zest for life which communicated itself to both staff and children. Her marked literary and dramatic talents were put to full use in the development of a broad and varied curriculum. The wonderful grounds with their lovely beck offered endless opportunities for studying nature on the spot, for picknicking, for learning to garden, for holding Brownie revels. By the thirties Oakdale was

Oakdale Preparatory School

bursting at the seams and needed more facilities, so in 1937 a large new wing was added. It provided a gymnasium with stage, additional dining-room space, and general accommodation for another 20 girls. During the war the building was not commandeered as College had been, and an extra house was acquired in Kent Road to meet the pressure of entry. In 1951 Miss Killingley was appointed as housemistress-in-charge. There were further additions to the premises and the numbers went over the 80 mark. Since nearly every Oakdaler proceeded to the big School most of the College entrants were from our own junior department, and this was very satisfactory. But the pattern of education in the country was changing, and by the sixties anxiety was being felt for the eventual future of Oakdale. The increasing trend for the 11-plus to enter their secondary school, and the lack of demand for entry at ten or earlier was becoming apparent. Oakdale was not entirely suitable for eleven-year-olds who needed more "senior" subjects, and the increasing cost of upkeep of the very large premises and grounds made the financial aspect worrying. In 1968 the governors came to the conclusion that Oakdale should be closed, and plans were therefore made to transfer the children to a house in Clarence Drive, and with the erection of four new class rooms on the playing field it was made possible to absorb them into the main school. Miss Killingley and Miss Dare, who had been in charge since 1950, moved up with them, as did several of the staff. It was a sad farewell to a place that had been much loved by generations of Oakdalers. There was naturally a sense of excitement among the children at the prospect of being part of the big school, but to those for whom Oakdale had been "home" for a long time, it was the end of a way of life.

The memories of childhood days are individual personal matters, but there were some special occasions at Oakdale that no-one who had been there could forget: the Summer evenings with the pets—rabbits, guinea pigs and hamsters, scampering on the lawn: the fireworks out in the eerie darkness of Guy Fawkes' night when the bursar ceremoniously came up from College to light the bonfire: the wonder and mystery of the Nativity Play in which everyone took part: the sheer magic of the Christmas party, conjuror included: Oakdale under snow: the beck in spate: the weekly walk up Kent Road for Sunday morning College Chapel: all part of the life that was Oakdale, and all now tucked away as memories—victims of changing circumstances.

The subsequent fate of the beautiful Oakdale premises is so extraordinary that space must be taken to recount it. In 1970 it was sold to a wealthy young businessman whose intention was that it should be extended and converted into a small select hotel. Once he had acquired it, however, he found it so attractive that he decided to keep it as his own private residence: he renamed it *Oakdale Manor* and spent a great deal of money on alterations and additions, including a fine outdoor swimming pool. Unfortunately, after three or four years, affairs began to go wrong for him, and he suddenly disappeared, leaving the country. The building stood unoccupied for a while before it was discovered by vandals, who found it a profitable target, and in spite of all the vigilance they could muster the police were unable to prevent them doing unbelievable damage. It was then put on the market and bought by a property developer whose intention was to demolish it and erect twelve detached houses on the land. Ironically it was a "listed building" and could not be pulled down without permission. It was at this point that preservation societies belatedly entered the fray, and after heated argument the matter was referred to the Ministry of the Environment. As a result of the enquiry the Ministry ruled, because of the state of delapidation, in favour of demolition. Accordingly, shortly afterwards the whole building was razed to the ground, reduced to vast piles of rubble, and so it has remained since then. The beck still flows undisturbed and the daffodils have given their annual display, but the rest is desolation.

At the top of the School we were realising that the upper sixth, now numbering between twenty-five and thirty, would be happier in a separate house. They were busy with highly competitive and exacting studies, and were worried that valuable time was being taken up by House matters for which, as House officials, they were responsible. Some of them, it had to be remembered, now even had the vote, and felt that though still at school they had already graduated into adulthood. The obvious premises suitable for the purpose were those occupied by Swinton in York Road, and so, during the summer holidays of 1971, it was refurnished to become an attractive upper sixth house. The name "Tower" which was found faintly carved into one of its gate posts seemed an entirely appropriate name to adopt for its new purpose, so Tower House it became once again. The House made an excellent start, thanks to its housemistress, Mrs Hutchings, the sister of Dr Ward, and also to Rhona Jordan, a very competent head of school, and it has continued to give the upper sixth a way of life which suits them very well. To complete the rearrangements, Swinton took up residence next to Armaclare in Clarence

1970 The Playing Field, showing new gymnasium, Memorial Room and junior classrooms

Drive, and the internal arrangements in all the Houses were organised so that the lower sixth henceforth took over the official positions including that of head of House, though the upper sixth provided most of the prefects of the school.

The considerable changes, in organisation, types of work, premises and much else, which had occurred during the last decade of the history of the School could not have taken place so smoothly had it not been for many long serving members of the staff who shared in the enterprises with such approval. Several of these now reached retirement age during this period. In 1960 had come the resignation on health grounds of Mr Stone who had been an efficient, kindly and greatly respected bursar since before the war. He was followed shortly afterwards by Commander Hine who continued to supervise the business and estate affairs until 1974. Miss Brock, after twenty-eight years as head of classics and an intellectual power in the staff room, was much missed by everyone, as was Miss Pease who had spent twenty-two patient and fruitful years presiding over the mathematics. Miss Sankey's years at college totalled over forty, in charge of the crafts and also for many years of the school charities. Miss Millen now left from the music department, and she and her elder sister Tron, who had been a pillar of strength at Oakdale, retired together to their flat in Harrogate. Miss Bacon, also in the music department since the war days, had carried on the organisation of the music corridors and time-table and she too retired after twenty-seven years at the school.

1970 The Chapel, showing new porch, the gymnasium and the Memorial Room
entrance.

Mention has several times been made of Miss Brown, and with her departure, after forty-five years, the College lost one of its most talented, colourful and best loved characters. Miss Brown had filled many rôles in her time, even being in charge of the school riding, in her day a largely attended and popular recreation. She was a first-class teacher of all types of domestic science, a brilliant organiser (of bazaars as well as in other spheres) and a perfectionist as well as an improviser. At Swinton she had borne the burden of the wartime housekeeping, and on the return to Harrogate she took over the task of controller of fabrics and furnishings and knew unerringly where every item of furniture and domestic equipment was located. As housemistress she had a remarkable insight into the working of the young mind and an influence on her girls that was outstanding. Miss Brown became a close friend of Miss Jones and her family, and was in fact with them during the last weeks of Lady Bell's life. Her anecdotes of "the old days" were legion, all recalled with pungent wit, and a style which was hers alone. She gave up Lincoln House in 1960 but stayed on a few years longer in a part-time capacity, of great esteem as an elder statesman.

Several of the College matrons were invaluable in providing the continuity in the house life, able too in many cases to welcome the daughters of their former girls, a source of reassurance and great pleasure to the "new" mothers. Miss Lawson of Armaclare was senior matron for many years: the school is indebted to her for her determination that, whatever the external pressures, high standards of behaviour and appearance must be maintained. Her thirty years of service were rewarded by the lasting affection of her girls. Miss Hinson in York, Mrs Davidson in Swinton, and Miss Wood in Lincoln each were in their Houses for over twenty years, and greatly respected by the parents who happily entrusted their daughters to their care. Dr John Ward, whose father had been school doctor and whose sisters and nieces pupils of College, also retired after many years of constant care of the health of the community.

Perhaps I should include myself in this list of people, as in length of service I outstripped them all. In 1970 the HCU celebrated the time of my Golden Jubilee by making me the Guest of Honour at a lovely party at their Reunion, a never-to-be-forgotten day. Two years later I too became fully retired.

It was indicative of the changing times that as the senior members of staff left they were frequently replaced by married teachers, sometimes part-time because of commitments to young children at home. Most staff were non-resident and it became quite customary to see a mistress arriving at school, not only carrying a satchel of corrected books, but also a shopping basket for use on the way home. Did the school suffer from the loss of those dedicated members of staff who had helped to pioneer it in its earlier years? Of course it did: and Harrogate College has been especially fortunate in the quality of those whose single-minded devotion had played such a part in shaping it. But it also gained. The new members of staff were equally of high calibre: they organised their busy lives with commendable efficiency, and brought into the staff room a reminder of the ordinary everyday problems that beset humanity outside the walls of a boarding school. They were good representatives of their profession and fitted in with the pattern forming in the girls' own minds as they themselves planned their careers in the modern world.

In 1973 College attained its eightieth birthday. There were the usual school functions in the summer, including Speech Day in the Royal Hall, but no special commemorations were arranged. The occasion was naturally over-shadowed by the knowledge that it would be Miss Todd's last speech day as she would be retiring later in the year.

Reaching the concluding pages of this history, I am so vividly conscious of the spell which Harrogate College has woven round its members, girls and staff alike. The "link" between past and present, stressed so earnestly by Miss Jones, has continued and strengthened. The Harrogate College Union, from its small beginnings, now has a membership of about 3 000 and a well organised constitution with a representative executive. Its activities, includ-ing its numerous gifts to the school, have already been referred to, as has also the work of several of its erstwhile officials. Amongst these Sybil Murray, Isabel Crawford, Rona Brown and Joyce Aikman have each in their turn been chairman. For the last twelve years Sheila Denton (Eastwood) has given especially valuable service as secretary/registrar, and has reorganised the business side of the Union while keeping in touch with its many members, and Joan Barnes (Hastewell) has been treasurer for over twenty years. Most of their time in office comes within the scope of this volume and so is acknowledged with appreciation.

Girls come and go, but the teachers, housemistresses and matrons have an influence on the succeeding generations which every girl recalls and treasures all her life. Many of the staff, both those from early times and those who have more recently retired, have been mentioned as they have come to mind, but as this book ends, in 1973, with Miss Todd's own retirement, she and I leave behind friends and associates who have already spent many years at school and whose contribution should not go unrecorded. There is Miss Graham, the school secretary, with her accumulated store of College information and her genuine personal interest in the girls. She it is who with her valuable knowledge has been so helpful in typing the manuscript of this book. Mrs W Wright, head of English studies (the College Birthday Book of Quotations, amongst many other things, will bring her to mind); Mrs Lowe, head of the history department, and frequently also a knowledgeable adviser on antiques; Miss Throup, our Russian expert; Jean Radford, the talented head of the art, with her former pupil Katherine Buist, now ardent in the crafts room, and also Miss Reynolds in charge of the needlework; Mrs N Wright and Mrs Dickinson in the science block—they who had the formidable task of refurnishing all the new rooms with their manifold equipment; Miss Robinson and Miss Smith whose play productions have given so much pleasure; Miss Haddow with her singing and orchestral work; Miss Kennedy and Miss Galt who work with such happiness and success on the games side. When we think of Oakdale we remember Miss Killingley and Miss Dare, Miss Hull, Miss Surtees and Miss Almond, who after their years there did so much to establish the junior section in the main school when the transition took place. Miss Green also came from Oakdale and became housemistress of Armaclare where she is much appreciated for all she does.

What an important part our long-serving housemistresses have always played in the College, each devoted to her House and influencing it by her own personality; Miss Linsdell with her specially large family in Lincoln; Mrs Boddy the founder of the new Clarence; Mrs Elliot, whose own two daughters were pupils, in Balliol: all these have gained the affection and confidence of very many girls. And finally there is Miss Crawford, head of the modern languages, who took over as Senior Mistress when I retired, and thus is grafted, probably for the rest of her life, to the affairs of Harrogate College; to her, and to all the so familiar colleagues I give my very good wishes.

The last section of the school's history is a record of Miss Todd's achievements as headmistress. All who were with her at College, staff and girls, recognised her notable leadership. It was not only the continuous growth in scholarship and in the buildings (her fund-raising speeches were irresistible) but to use a trite phrase, everyone liked her, and with this attribute the leadership of a big and varied community was assured. We never found that troubled parents or a difficult teacher, a naughty girl, or even discontented workers in kitchen or estate, did not emerge from her room feeling better than when they went in. The times are too close to assess the last twenty years, but a fine school has been handed on to the new headmistress, Mrs Lawrance, with the good wishes of everyone for its continued success, and the triumphant attainment of its centenary.

Postscript by Miss Todd

It seems to me that as time passes, future readers of this book will regret that the story gives so little information about the writer who has been responsible for its production, and I have sought, and been given, permission to remedy this.

Dorothy Hewlett was educated at St Swithin's, Winchester and is a science graduate of St Andrews University. It was in those early days that Chance first took a hand, for there at St Andrews was begun a life-long friendship with a fellow student, Christian Robertson (Buist). Christian, a former head girl of Harrogate College, had been "booked" by Miss Jones to return in due course as a member of staff, and when the time came for this to happen she made enquiry as to the possibility of a vacancy in the science department for her friend. Miss Jones, on consideration, decided that a post could be made available, but that it would be to teach science, botany, and some Latin, with three afternoons on the games field coaching lacrosse! In spite of somewhat scant experience in two of these subjects, Miss Hewlett, nothing daunted, accepted, and thus it was that in 1920 the long association with Harrogate College began.

It was Miss Hewlett's good fortune in this, her first, post, to come under the influence of a headmistress such as Miss Jones. It proved to be a fruitful apprenticeship, and before long Miss Jones was appreciating the calibre of this young mistress and was increasing her responsibilities. In 1934 she became housemistress of York House, a position which she held until 1962, and in 1940 she was appointed, this time by Miss Jacob, to be Senior Mistress. It was in this latter capacity that her valuable organising powers were in evidence. The final few years were spent in part-time work, and she retired in 1972.

In these few sentences is condensed a lifetime of happy and rewarding service to the school, and it is a great joy that it should now be rounded off by the writing of this book. Much could be written of Miss Hewlett's personal attributes, but that is not my brief. Suffice it to say that to those of us who know her she stands for all that is best in the public school tradition, and fortunate indeed has been the school to which she has given her undivided loyalty over the years.

M W S Todd

Heads of School 1901–73

1901	M Blackburn		
1902	M Shaw		
1903	N Duncan		
1904	W Davey		
1905	W Holloway		
1906	I Russell	O Elliot	
1907	O Elliot	R Arden	
1908	G Wilkes		
1909	G Wilkes		
1910	A Bowden	A McGlashan	
1911	V Gould	M Broadbent	
1912	M Broadbent	K Herdman	
1913	L Burgoyne		
1914	E Herdman		
1915	C Robertson		
1916	M Watherston		
1917	M Luis		
1918	M Waghorn	M Willis	
1919	S Toler		
1920	S Toler		
1921	K Moulsdale		
1922	G Laird		
1923	A Frazer		
1924	E Risk		
1925	K Stockdale		
1926	G Plant		
1927	K Fell		
1928	I Glenny		
1929	R Heal		
1930	C Fell		
1931	K Merry	M Edmonds	
1932	V Lock		
1933	E Myott		
1934	M Howell	M Gillhespy	
1935	B Brownridge	R Turnbull	
1936	V Tunbridge		
1937	L Macleod	C Jenkins	
1938	E Newton		
1939	G Allen	K Little	
1940	D Heatley-Spencer	M Phillips	
1941	P Hampton		
1942	M Ashforth		

1943	M Field		
1944	S Grant		
1945	A Griffiths		
1946	J Fraser		
1947	M Bromley		
1948	E Sharp		
1949	E Atkinson	M McLuckie	
1950	E Jagoe		
1951	R Hole		
1952	R Harrison		
1953	M King		
1954	J Hazzledine		
1955	J Mehew	F Norwell	
1956	M Ballard	F Hamilton-Turner	
1957	G Jopling		
1958	A Hannah		
1959	P Crowder		
1960	E Harrison		
1961	G Egginton		
1962	J Cutting		
1963	A Grundy		
1964	F Denby		
1965	S Leslie		
1966	D Calder		
1967	Y Miller		
1968	P Wingate		
1969	S Twist	J Irwin	
1970	S Pattinson		
1971	R Jordan		
1972	P Bevan		
1973	P Wilkinson		

COMPLETING THE LIST TO THE PRESENT DAY

1974	S Rountree
1975	J Metcalfe
1976	S Dagg
1977	L Horler
1978	E Shelton
1979	S Davies
1980	L Benson

This record tells the story of former times, and its readers will be interested to know the names of those who, at the end of 1980, as the book goes to press, hold office in the present organisation of Harrogate College.

GOVERNORS OF HARROGATE COLLEGE:

Mrs C E W Sheepshanks, JP   Chairman
Mrs B T Aikman
Mrs J L Kennerley Bankes, BSc   HCU Representative
Sir Richard K Denby, LLB
Mrs N Grieve
Miss I Hindmarsh, JP MA
Mr R G Ikin MA
Lady Ingilby
The Very Rev Brandon D Jackson, LLB
Mr O R Johnston MA
Colonel G A Leech, TD, C Eng, FI Mun E, FIHE
Mr G Lingwood, FIA
Mrs P H C Walker

Chairman of the Allied Schools: Mr D E Bateman CA, MA

Secretary to the Governors and General Manager of
the Allied Schools: Mr W Clowes

Headmistress: Mrs J C Lawrance, MA (Oxon)

Senior Mistress: Miss I A J D Crawford, BA
Senior Housemistress: Miss M Morley
Chaplain: Rev R Kent BA
Bursar: Lt Colonel R E P Ince

Chairman of Harrogate College Union: Mrs Marlow (Rita Turnbull)
HCU Secretary: Mrs Wheatcroft (Betty Gray)
HCU Treasurer: Mrs Hastewell (Joan Barnes) BSc

Drawn by Carol Harte as a Christmas card for the Princess Royal after her visit

"The hour of departure has arrived, and we go our ways"

PLATO

← PATH TO SWINTON

5.

6.

1.

3.

SWINTON HOUSE 1946

changed to
TOWER HOUSE 1971
for U.VI. form

HARROGATE COLLE

CH

GRASSINGTON
  1946
(Headmistress)

MAIN BUILDING 1904, NEW WING 1925

CLARENCE 1911
changed to
SANATORIUM 1975

RYLSTONE & FAWCETT
changed to SWINTON 1971 (STAFF)

ARMACLARE 1917

Additional buildings since 1959 are indicated by numbers on the dr

1. JUNIOR FORM ROOMS 1960

5. Nos. 17–overflow for SWINTON
    and 19–MUSIC DEPT. } acquired 1962

3. BI
and 4. SC

6. LIBRARY EXTENSION 1968